THE DRONE EATS WITH ME

THE DRONE
EATS
WITH ME

A Gaza Diary

ATEF ABU SAIF

Beacon Press
Boston

BEACON PRESS
Boston, Massachusetts
www.beacon.org

Beacon Press books
are published under the auspices of
the Unitarian Universalist Association of Congregations.

Originally published as *The Drone Eats with Me: Diaries from
a City Under Fire*, by Comma Press.

26 25 24 23   8 7 6 5 4 3 2

This book is printed on acid-free paper that meets the uncoated paper
ANSI/NISO specifications for permanence as revised in 1992.

Text design and composition by Kim Arney

The excerpt from Mahmoud Darwish's poem "The Eternity of Cactus," from *Why
Did You Leave the Horse Alone?*, is courtesy of Archipelago Books.

Sixteen of these diary entries originally appeared in newspapers and websites during
the summer of 2014: "Day Seven" (12 July) appeared in *Guernica* as "The Children
Have Barely Slept" (https://guernicamag.com, 31 July 2014). "I Do Not Want to Be a
Number" (22 July) first appeared in *Slate* (http://slate.com, 23 July 2014). "We Wait
Each Night for Death to Knock at the Door" (24 July) first appeared in the *Sunday
Times* (UK) (27 July 2014). The entries for 23–26 July appeared in an edited form as
"Life Under Fire: The Diary of a Palestinian" in the *Guardian* (UK) (28 July 2014), and
for 27 July to 3 August as "Eight Days in Gaza: A Wartime Diary" (op-ed) in the *New
York Times* (4 August 2014). Part of the afterword was also published in the *Guardian*
(17 December 2014).

Library of Congress Cataloging-in-Publication Data
Names: Abu Saif, Atef, author.
Title: The drone eats with me : a Gaza diary / Atef Abu Saif.
Description: Boston, Mass. : Beacon Press, 2016. | Includes bibliographical references.
Identifiers: LCCN 2015044062| ISBN 9780807049105 (paperback) |
    ISBN 9780807049112 (ebook)
Subjects: LCSH: Abu Saif, Atef.| Palestinian Arabs--Gaza
    Strip—Biography. | Gaza Strip--Social conditions. | Gaza Strip—Politics
    and government.
Classification: LCC DS110.G3 A288 2016 | DDC 953.1—dc23
LC record available at http://lccn.loc.gov/2015044062

To my little Jaffa
—may your future be better than my present.

IT BEGINS

WHEN IT COMES, it brings with it a smell, a fragrance even. You learn to recognize it as a kid growing up in these narrow streets. You develop a knack for detecting it, tasting it in the air. You can almost see it. Like a witch's familiar, it lurks in the shadows, follows you at a distance wherever you go. If you retain this skill, you can tell that it's coming—hours, sometimes days, before it actually arrives. You don't mistake it. بر‍ح. *Harb.* War.

I'm sitting in front of Abu Annas's house with three of our friends—Tarik, Sohail, and Abdallah. Abu Annas has been a headmaster for fifteen years now at the camp's Ahmad al-Shokairi High School, although I've known him since the First Intifada.[1] He lives just a two-minute walk from my father's place, in the same refugee camp I grew up in. The night is warm. Two shade trees stand in front of the house.

Abu Annas and Tarik are playing backgammon, from time to time breaking away from their game to contribute to the wider conversation. The sound of the dice rattling against the wooden board always mesmerizes me slightly. I've never played backgammon. I merely love the spectacle of dice bouncing along the wood and ricocheting off the back board. An aging blue Sony radio sits between us, playing a classic Fayza Ahmad[2] song. "Oh Mother, the moon is at the door, lighting candles. Shall I lock the door or open it?" Abu Annas has kept the radio in good condition since the 1970s, still wrapped in a brown leather casing it came with.

All five of us around the table were born in wartime—as Gazans, you don't get much choice about it. The crowded refugee camp we grew up in, known to Gazans as "Jabalia"[3]—once a field of tents, then a forest of shacks, now a jungle of high-rise apartment blocks crammed tightly together—has been beset by wars for as long as we've all been alive. Since 1948—before that in fact, since the British mandate began in 1917—Gaza has barely gone ten years without a war; sometimes it's as little as two between each one. So everyone carries their own memories of conflict: wars stand as markers in a Gazan's life: there's one planted firmly in your childhood, one or two more in your adolescence, and so on . . . they toll the passing of time as you grow older like rings in a tree trunk. Sadly, for many Gazans, one of these wars will also mark life's end. Life is what we have in between these wars.

Tonight, another one is starting. SMS news updates interrupt the evening's conversation, with innocent little pings, more and more and more frequently as the night progresses, as we flinch to read them, more and more nervously. The last sustained attack on the Strip was back in November 2012 and lasted for eight days. The one before that—dubbed "Cast Lead" by the Israelis—ran from December 2008 to January 2009 and lasted for twenty-three days. How many days will this one last? How will it compare to previous assaults? These are the questions I want us to be discussing, but for Abu Annas, at least, it isn't even certain that war is coming. "It will only be a small incursion," he says, "a limited one."

Zohdi, Abu Annas's second son, who is also my barber, prepares the *shisha* for all of us. When I see him I reach up out of habit and feel my hair and stubble: it's only been three days since they were last trimmed. Zohdi's shop is right beside Abu Annas's house and seeing him appear in the doorway with a flash of steel in his hand makes me think I'm about to feel razor against skin. Then I see that it's just the steel tongs for the charcoal.

Tarik, a veteran workers' rights activist, leans over the shisha to blow on the coals, saying that all indicators point to war. Sohail is more skeptical about it. Sohail spent much of his early life in Israeli prisons, having been a local PLO leader in the camp, and served in Fatah's secret militia during the '80s. He insists that we are already in the holy month of Ramadan and that full-on war, at least, will have to be delayed until the end of the month, although a controlled "escalation of tension" may be a feature of the next few weeks. Abdallah, who holds a PhD in psychology, shares this reading.

Me?

Well, I tell them, I can smell it. I sense it drawing in.

As it turns out, it has arrived already, before we even started this conversation.

At around 9 p.m. this evening, a drone attacked a group of people near Beit Hanoun, two miles north of Jabalia Camp. No one was injured. Half an hour later another drone fired on three people on the street in the western side of Gaza City. At the time, these were reported as one-offs, the way bad traffic accidents would be. Such things happen now and then—usually a lot more than half an hour apart, of course, but two drone strikes don't make a war. This is what the radio calls an "escalation in tension." Then the presenter goes back to his scheduled program on youth problems in Gaza. His guest for the discussion starts to discuss the despair that hangs over so many young people, especially with regard to their futures; how trapped they feel being unable to travel, study, or make a career outside of the Strip. Then suddenly, at about 11 p.m., the guest is cut off and a nationalist song starts playing. The mood on the radio changes completely.

A few minutes later, Abu Annas's mobile pings with information on a third attack. "Two young men killed in attack in Bureij Camp."[4] We look at each other. This is no "escalation in tension."

A moment later, the war introduces itself properly. We hear an explosion, some way to the north, echoing across the city. Hearing a bomb in real life, for the first time in a couple of years, is like having a PTSD flashback. It jolts you to exactly where you were two years ago, five years ago, four decades ago, to the most recent, or very first time you heard one. As the noise of this new explosion subsides it's replaced by the inevitable whir of a drone, sounding so close it could be right beside us. It's like it wants to join us for the evening and has pulled up an invisible chair.

Because it's Ramadan and we have to be awake for the *suhoor*⁵—which at this time of year is around 3:30 a.m.—we spend most nights staying up, talking, smoking shisha and eating Ramadan specialties: sweets and pastries like *awama*,⁶ *kenafeh*,⁷ and baklava. Being the height of summer, it's also far better to spend this time in front of the house, under a tree, than sweat it out indoors.

When we first sat down tonight, scores of boys passed us singing Ramadan hymns and beating on plastic boxes, turning them into drums: nice hymns, the same ones I used to sing at their age. It's a tradition that starts three days before Ramadan and runs all the way to Eid; I imagine it makes any Palestinian man—devout or not—warm with nostalgia to hear them.

But now the street is empty; the sound of the explosions has grown louder. Everyone prefers to be inside. Tarik suggests that we go too, but Abu Annas insists: "Don't worry, it's normal." We know it's normal, but we have to go. Hanna, my wife, rings me saying that the explosions are everywhere, I need to be with her. Her voice trembles: "The kids are sleeping." I know she is afraid to be on her own right now.

Tarik drives me back quickly. I live in the Saftawi district, to the west of Jabalia Camp. All the inhabitants of the districts around the camp originate from inside it. Jabalia is the largest refugee camp in all of Palestine, home to over one hundred thousand Gazans in only 1.4 square kilometers. It's probably most famous as the setting of countless confrontations between occupying Israeli forces and

Palestinians, in particular during the First Intifada, which broke out in its narrow streets. Now, with its increased population, it has spawned new districts around its outskirts: places like Alami, Tel Azaatar, Salaheen, Beir al-Na'aja, and Saftawi. In many ways these all belong to the camp; they are its children.

Tarik is worried that a war in the summer, especially during Ramadan, will be hard on the people. Before dropping me off, he reminds me of our meeting tomorrow, two hours before sunset. Every evening, since the start of Ramadan, Tarik and I have driven out to a small farm his family owns to the west of Beit Lahia, where he grows fruit and vegetables. We spend the last two hours of sunlight there, before *iftar* (literally, the "breakfast"). The hardest hours of fasting are those last ones just before the iftar, so it's good to have a distraction.

I smile at his reminder.

"What if this is war?" I ask.

"This can't be war."

Inside, I find Hanna perched on the edge of the sofa, listening to the news, rigid with worry. Even her eyes tell me, "This is war." I make coffee and set out a few pieces of *katayef*[8] for when the children wake. With Hanna, I begin the same conversation that every single adult in Gaza is having right now with someone else: What if this really is war? How long will it last? Will it be harder than the previous ones? Will we survive? Which of our loved ones is going to be lost?

Hanna shouts my name, saying I need to wake the kids up for the suhoor.

It is 3:30 a.m. Monday, 7 July 2014. A date to remember.

Monday, 7 July

THE BEAT OF
DRUMS AND BOMBS

SINCE MIDNIGHT, THE SHELLING and bombing hasn't let up. Tonight, the *musaharati* is nowhere to be seen. The musaharati is one of the oldest features of the holy month of Ramadan; he paces through the streets waking people to take their suhoor. You can't imagine Ramadan without him. He is usually an older man, patrolling the neighborhood with a drum, often with a lantern swinging below it. In a fine, well-trained voice he sings a particular song to rouse us.

Every neighborhood of the camp has its own musaharati. And at the end of the month, he knocks on your door asking for a contribution—money or a gift of food—in return for his service.

Tonight, in my district, a group of young men seem to have collectively assumed the role, striking up at around 2:40 a.m. This is a new phenomenon. They sing the suhoor song and insert the names of almost every person in the street so it becomes a private call for him or her to wake up.

They stand in front of our apartment block and start to sing the names of the people living in it. We only moved into this building three years ago so in the first two Ramadans, they failed to include any of our names on the list. At the start of Ramadan, I had asked the musaharati to update the records so my four boys' names could be included—Talal, Mostafa, Naeem, Yasser. As my youngest, Jaffa, is only nineteen months old, she has no awareness of this, so she hasn't been included yet.

As children, having your name sung by the musaharati is a genuine thrill. Knowing they were finally going to be included this year was a source of real excitement for my boys, and on the first night of Ramadan, they barely slept in anticipation of it. The thrill of hearing their names lasted for the first week. Now they are not getting up early and standing by the window in anticipation of it anymore. When the suhoor time comes, I have to wake them up myself. Naeem asks sluggishly: "Have the musaharatis been already?" They haven't and I know they probably won't anymore, so there's no point in the boys getting up early to hear them. But I don't want to worry Naeem, so I just say he missed them. He believes me, for now.

It's mid-afternoon and in the eighteen hours since the raids began, eleven people have been killed and scores of others injured. Every hour the number of victims increases. When we woke up today, Hanna and the kids spent an hour or so talking about the previous war and our memories of it. This will be the third war my children have witnessed in five years. The 2008–2009 war came quite out of the blue by Israeli standards. On that cold morning in December, I was giving a lecture series to a group of young men and women about human rights and democracy, on the other side of town. The human rights center I was teaching in was close to Gaza's main military and policing compound, a place called Jawazat. This compound was one of the first places in the Strip to come under heavy attack. I was in the middle of a lecture when we heard it and all the students started to shout.

We abandoned the class and all headed up onto the roof to see what was happening. All of Gaza was shaking. There were explosions in every direction. A column of smoke rose to the sky wherever you looked. I knew Talal and Mostafa would be at school and Hanna phoned, terrified, saying someone should bring them home. Before she hung up, we were both relieved to hear the doorbell ring, and to her joy, she opened it to see the two of them, home safe. This was 27 December 2008 and that war lasted until 18 January 2009.

The next war broke out on 14 November 2012, dubbed "Pillar of Defense" by the Israelis. It began with a raid that killed, among others, a prominent military figure.[*] At the time of the first strike, I was at the Saraya crossroads.[1] I was just crossing the road, heading towards the Karawan Café—my favorite café in Gaza—when suddenly there was a huge explosion in one of the backstreets behind the Saraya and opposite the Gaza Municipal Park. There was no warning of this attack; everyone in the street just went into autopilot, remembering instinctively what to do, and where to run to, in an air raid. Before the ambulances could get to the scene, F16s and drones started to rain missiles down on the district.

Will this war be different? No one can tell. The rhythm of the explosions last night and all through today seemed faster than before, heavier. As we talked, we allowed ourselves the indulgence of a few comparisons. One of the differences, so far, is that the current assault broke out gradually—we could not tell, last night at Abu Annas's house, whether it was war or just an escalation in tension, an incursion, a shot over our bow.

The first rule of wartime is don't go out. Or at least, only when you have to. The children, of course, must never leave the building.

My sister Amina is scheduled to have an operation this afternoon in the Beit Hanoun hospital. On my way to visit her, I hear a handful of explosions coming from the north of the town, and on the road to the hospital, I see a patch of rubble where a house had once stood, on the banks of the Wadi Beit Hanoun.[2] This house had been damaged in the 2012 war and had never been properly rebuilt. Now the drone has finished the job.

---

[*]Ahmed Jabari, chief of the Gaza military wing of Hamas.

Back at the house, Hanna tells me we need to stock up on vegetables, meat, chicken, and the like, and everyone else will be doing the same. So I head back out to the camp's *souq*. But before I get to Saftawi Square, a roar of explosions sounds somewhere to the north. I run for shelter under the porch of a nearby building. More explosions reverberate a few minutes later. After fifteen minutes, it seems to stop completely and silence returns, except for the whir of the drones.

When I get home, we start to prepare the food to break the fast. Even the kids join Hanna and me in the kitchen and offer to help. Making yourself busy at a time like this helps. Of the children, only Talal and Mostafa are fasting. And they're starving, impatient for the sun to plunge under the horizon.

Suddenly Hanna says, "Don't tell me you're planning to go to your father's neighborhood after the breakfast?" Actually, I had intended to. I tell her I have to see my father and family but she insists it's too dangerous. I reply: "All of Gaza is dangerous."

FEEDING TIMES

THERE IS A strange irony to these raids. The heaviest passages in the round-the-clock bombardment seem to be at the two times of the day when we're serving food—the suhoor and the iftar. Then the raids go crazy. They rain down on all sides—it's like a monsoon that we've just escaped from, to eat. The building shakes. The horizon dances in the window. You don't know if it's you or the whole of Gaza that's moving. Explosions can be heard intermittently all day and night, but when we set the table at 3:30 a.m. for the suhoor, and at 7:40 p.m. for the iftar, it feels like there's a fanfare being played, especially for the food. As the sun is just below the horizon at both these times, the dusk sky lights up with the bombs and is colored by the red and blue tongues of fire.

This morning, as I prepare the suhoor with Hanna, there is a sudden explosion—somewhere nearby, probably the Maqosi area, which is a cluster of tall buildings in the Nasser quarter of Gaza City. Then more attacks. Mostafa wakes up by himself—the thunder of the shells doing what the musaharatis would have. He wakes his brothers, leaving only Jaffa to sleep through it all. Afterwards, as I lay awake in bed, unable to sleep due to the ever-present whir of a drone, I reflect on how the children are already adjusting to the logic of the war, learning things I learned so long ago.

In the afternoon, I play cards with the whole family. Just to kill some time.

The army seems to be targeting residential buildings only. F16s have only hit houses today, razing them to street level. In east Khan Younis, a house belonging to the Abadallah family was completely destroyed. Many others in Gaza City and Rafah have been hit. Two mosques as well. But the greatest tragedy of the day was the killing of the Kawari' family in Khan Younis. An Israeli F16 attacked the family home while the children and parents were preparing the iftar. The F16 wasn't willing to let a family be happy together, to get on with life despite the war. It decided to put an end to such things.

At 6 p.m., a young man was driving his *toktok*¹ when a rocket struck him directly, leaving a crater in the ground and unimaginable remains. This was northeast of Jabalia Camp, near the Sheikh Zayed Housing Project. A young man who sold kids' food—sweets, chocolates, crisps—became, in the eyes of the drone operator, a valid target, a danger to Israel. Every single human being in Gaza, whether walking on foot, riding a bicycle, steering a *toktok*, or driving a car, is a threat to Israel now. We're all guilty until proven otherwise, and how are we ever going to do that, whether alive or not? Your innocence doesn't matter—you have to abandon that. Survival is your only care.

After the iftar, I visit my father. He is busy performing the Ramadan evening prayers, so I call in on Faraj, a childhood friend who lives very close to my dad. Faraj suggests that we go and watch the Germany versus Brazil World Cup semifinal at Ayman's place. Ayman is a friend of ours who's deeply fond of football. World War Three wouldn't prevent him from catching a big game like this. Ayman's house in Jabalia Camp has a large empty room at the front with a TV. We arrive to find over thirty people assembled to watch the match. The place looks like a café. My son Mostafa is also mad about football. He texts me to ask if I'll take him to watch the match somewhere. But it's too dangerous for him—the two of us wouldn't be able to move quickly enough if something started. Last week, before the war broke out, I took the four boys to watch the last-sixteen game between Germany and Algeria. In a huge café, with great big plasma screens on all sides, the boys spent hours shouting and dancing in support of Algeria. Afterwards, I promised to take them to the same café for the next round of games: the quarter finals, then the semis. . . . Some promises you're allowed to break.

After the game—a momentous 7-1 drubbing of Brazil—I stop by to see Abu Annas on my way home. "He's not in," Zohdi tells me at the door of his shop next door, a pair of scissors in his hands. "He's playing chess with his neighbor." Then he looks at me and comments on how hirsute I'm becoming. He offers to give me a shave and trim, right there. I tell him, "No—I'll grow my beard and my hair till the war ends." He laughs and tells me there is no connection between a war and one man's hair. I smile: "There's a big connection!"

He opens and closes the scissors and says, "Yalla!"*

"La,"† I say.

---

* "Let's go."
† "No."

A GHOST OF A CITY

IT FEELS LIKE it's going to be a long one. No one is talking about a truce. In previous wars, talks about cease-fires started on the first day. Now we're into the fourth day and no one has even used the word. Small demonstrations have taken place in a few European cities, but there's been no real mention of the war by international politicians. Even in the Arab states, there's been no demonstrations, only condemnation. Such words and protests don't help much, but they do give you a sense that someone out there is thinking of you, that someone, though helpless, cares about the killing and believes you have a right to live in peace.

One question that my boy Naeem asks is: "Are we going to go to school after Ramadan?" He loves school. He tells me that he misses his classmates. I can't imagine why he thinks it's going to go on for so long. He says he has a feeling that something is going wrong in this war. I smile and reassure him: "Don't be silly, the war is going to end tomorrow or the day after, and everything's going to be OK." He replies that I've said "tomorrow" every day so far. "Someday very soon it will end," I tell him. "Soon."

"Before the schools term starts again."

"Of course."

"Will we be able to go to school if the war hasn't ended then?"

"Don't worry about the first day of term!" I laugh—I have such a geek for a son! "It will be over by then."

I would like someone to reassure me that I'm not lying to my child, that I am telling him the truth, or even that I'm telling him what I believe, at least. No one can, as I cannot myself.

Last night six people from the Hamad family in Beit Hanoun were killed in an air raid.* Among them, two children and two women. I try to call Akram, a close friend of mine from the same family, to make sure he is OK, but I don't manage to get through. The mobile network is down. This is often the case during drone attacks. It interferes with their communications, so the Israelis simply disable them.

This morning, we woke up to the sound of heavy assaults all across Saftawi and from the nearby district of Beir al-Na'aja. By noon, some twenty-one people had been killed already, among them an eighteen-month-old baby by the name of Nariman Abdel Ghafour,[1] and a two-and-a-half-year-old boy, Mohammad Malake.[2] The latter was killed with his mother while sitting on her lap. She couldn't protect him.

Are things going to carry on like this? I wonder. It seems very few people outside Gaza care.

When the kids finally go to sleep tonight, Hanna and I sit in the dark. Akram texts to say he has escaped the fate of his cousins in Beit Hanoun and made it safely into Gaza City. Normally, right now, we'd be watching one of Hanna's favorite Ramadan TV series, but there's no electricity. One of the rules of our house is no candles. Hanna is very strict about this. She doesn't want to wake up with fire devouring the children, she says. Since Israel bombed

---

*Killed were Hafez Hamad (thirty-seven), his wife, Suha Hamad (thirty-one), mother, Fawzia Hamad (seventy), brothers Ibrahim (thirty-five) and Mahdi (forty-one), and Mahdi's teenage daughter, Dina (age unknown). They were survived by Hafez (eleven), his injured brother Noor (five), and sister Lamis (five months), who were taken to hospital. (Asmaa Al-Ghoul, "Israel Strikes Family Having Coffee," *Al-Monitor*, 13 July 2014, http://www.al-monitor.com/pulse /originals/2014/07/israel-gaza-strike-kills-hamad-family.html.)

the Gaza Power Station seven years ago, reduced capacity and fuel shortages have meant Gaza is subjected to rolling blackouts.[3] Many catastrophes have subsequently befallen Gazans as they adjusted to a nineteenth-century way of living for at least eight hours of every day. Whole families have died in their sleep because of house fires started by candles. Like many families, we are able to afford an electricity generator, which, until recently, we kept on the balcony. But many accidents have been caused by misuse of these generators. The stories you hear are terrifying: explosions, fires, people getting mangled or electrocuted. After about a year, we decided to ban the use of our generator. It was dangerous. No candles and no generator means we have to accept darkness half the time. It is better than third-degree burns or an electric shock.

I know I will have to revisit this conversation with Hanna and try to persuade her to let me use candles at night for my writing. Only for writing. But then I start to imagine my papers catching fire, so I leave it for now, try to accept the darkness.

Without a TV, we stand by the window and watch Gaza, together. Fields of darkness spread out in all directions. The ghost of a city. The only lights are those of the drones and F16s hovering above it all.

BEIT
HANOUN

JABALIA

GAZA
CITY

BEIT
LAHIA

DEIR AL BALAH

KHAN
YOUNIS

KHUZA'A

RAFAH

Gaza City

Thursday, 10 July

WATCHING THE GAME

LAST NIGHT, WHILE my friends and I were watching the second semifinal between Netherlands and Argentina at my friend Ayman's place in the Kasasib area of the camp, another group of men were doing the same in a small café on the beach of Khan Younis. Their café was called Sahar Al-Layali, which means "staying up all night."[1] Like us, they were smoking shisha, cheering for their favorite team, complaining about big players making obvious mistakes, putting their hands on their heads at near misses and close calls. They could hardly have been thinking about that gunship out there in the darkness, watching them, or the anger it stored, as they cheered and shouted at the match. They could hardly have imagined its maw, the gaping mouth of its gun turret, salivating with hunger for their souls.*

Six of them were killed instantly, another fourteen maimed. Their blood must have covered the sand all around the café, then slowly started to trickle down to the sea. The red charcoals from the top of their shisha pipes must have blown up into the night sky,

---

*The victims of this attack were later reported to be Mohammed Khalid Qanann (twenty-five) and his brother Ibrahim Qanann (twenty-four), Mohammad Al-'Aqad (twenty-four), Suleiman al-Astal (fifty-five), Hamdi Kamel Sawali, Ahmad Sawali, Ibrahim Sawali, Salim Sawali, Ahmed al-Astal, and Musa al-Astal (ages all unknown).

then descended, still flaming, like falling stars. By the morning, three of the injured had joined the dead. They never lived to watch the final of the World Cup. None of their favorite players will ever hear about their death.

I wake at around 9 a.m. to the news that over thirty people were killed in the small hours of the night. The casualty rate grows steadily every day. More people are killed by single strikes in groups; in fives, sevens, nines. Individuals aren't the targets, but residences, family houses. They're bombed until there's nothing left.

Around midday, a thunderous detonation shakes the house. It seems a car has been destroyed, very close to Saftawi Square, east of us. Three of the passengers were killed. The fourth is in a critical condition.

A few hours later, Hanna, the kids, and I decide on a way of making the most of the few hours of electricity we have left, as a family. We gather round the TV for a few hours to watch cartoons: *SpongeBob SquarePants* and *Gumball*. You need to forget about the world outside, or at least pretend you have the superpower of forgetfulness. About an hour later, an explosion rocks the building from the east, the flash lighting up the room a split second before the sound. A moment later, a thick cloud of sand is gliding across the lounge from the window behind us. An orange orchard it seems, a hundred meters away, has been attacked. The trees flew into the air then fell on top of each other, a jumble of broken boughs. When I inspect the damage later that evening, I see that several tons of sand seem to have been removed from underneath the orchard entirely. Part of it now coats the floor and furniture of our lounge.

It feels, right now, as if we are all living in a cloud of slow-moving sand: we inch forward through it, nervously, not seeing a yard in front of us, and when we come across a pile of orange trees, scattered at our feet like an assassin's victims, we know that we are lucky. They were mistaken for us. Death is so close that it doesn't see you anymore. It mistakes you for trees, and trees for you. You pray in thanks for this strange fog, this blindness.

Yasser asks me if I can go out and buy him an ice cream from a shop he knows has opened on Saftawi Square. "It's closed," I tell him.

"Will it open after iftar?" he asks.

I promised to take the kids to this shop; it's a new branch of a chain of Jabalia ice cream stores run by the Abu Zatoun family—another promise I have to break. Yasser then asks, "But you'll take us when the *zanana*† stops?"

"It's a deal," I say.

As I tuck him in later that night, I can tell he's keeping his ears peeled for the moment when the whir of the drones stops. He falls asleep, the shop stays closed, the drone hovers.

---

† Onomatopoeic word for "drone" peculiar to the Gazan dialect.

Friday, 11 July

FLOODLIT CITY

THERE ARE FLOODLIGHTS, lightning strikes, searchlights . . . lights on all sides.

Flashes.

Thunderous explosions.

The building shakes. The glass panes of each window shatter, one by one. The frames creak into new positions, their metal splitting.

Darkness is a ghoul that grinds and chews and gnaws at our calm. Worry courses through our veins. Uncertainty bites into our rest.

Another explosion, nearer than the others. Then the sound of windows blowing out, scattering shards across the floor. I flinch and can't tell if some of the fragments have implanted into me, or if I've imagined it. I run to the children but they are still sleeping safely. I turn on the radio. Turn it up loud.

The reporter Mohamed al-Battish declares: "More explosions in al-Zarka district. Two missiles."

The reporter Mohamad al-Ashkar: "An explosion in al-Tiwam quarter."

What about the explosion that just blew out our windows?!

A third reporter: "I am now standing in the western part of north Gaza. Israeli warplanes have attacked a building near to the Karama Hospital, east of the Karama Towers."

It seems he's referring to the same attack as Al-Ashkar but from a different perspective.

A fourth reporter: "The sky is full of F16s, flying at low altitudes. More activity reported off the coast of Beit Lahia, warships assembling."

Another reporter with a hoarse voice: "Flames are still engulfing the port of Gaza. I am being told now of another attack in Ahmad Yassen Street. Yes . . . yes . . . two missiles have struck a residence, leaving it severely damaged."

Some TV channels carry on blissfully, seemingly untouched by the chaos. A Ramadan drama serial is playing on MBC.[1] I try, despite everything, to follow it, despite the fireballs of lava whizzing through the air outside the window. Passing the time is the most challenging of tasks in such moments, a true mission: to wrap distraction around your panic, smother it in frivolous entertainment; to silence your fear by trying to focus on the predictable ending of a cheap Ramadan TV serial with a terrible plot. A hard mission for a hard time. Nonetheless, you try.

More floodlights.

Floodlights.

Flashes.

Thunder.

A missile strikes and I feel like I've been thrown ten centimeters into the air above the sofa I'm lying on. The remote control, which a minute ago I held in my right hand, clatters to the floor, the parts dispersing in all directions. Then total darkness. I'm scared to get up. I think the TV is going to fall from its perch and smash. I switch on the little torch.

Hanna and the children have been sleeping in the corridor, opposite the kitchen. A few days ago we set down mattresses and bedding in the corridor that runs through the middle of our apartment—the furthest room from the outside wall. We figure it's the safest place in the building. At the sound of this last explosion, they all jump up from their mattresses, looking around in panic. I run into the corridor and see the children's expressions immediately. Glass is everywhere, the full length of the hall. I can't work out which window it's come from. I grab the children, check each one in turn to see if they've been cut anywhere, looking for lacerations, for blood. I scan every part of them at speed, their hair, their arms, their feet. I can see tiny pieces of glass glinting on all their pillows and bedsheets. After a while, I figure out that the glass must have come from the door of the bathroom balcony. But it has flown right through the bathroom and up the corridor to get here.

I look into the eyes of little Jaffa and feel scared for her but try to retain some calm in my eyes, for both our sakes.

The reporters continue to fill the apartment with breaking news.

One reporter: "A missile has hit an area of farmland belonging to the Mokat family."

Another reporter: "A wing of al-Wafa Hospital east of Gaza City has also been hit."

A piercing light spreads across the whole city momentarily.

I see balls of flame falling from a great height.

I see points of lava flying in, horizontally, from the west, the sea.

More floodlights. More explosions.

The building shakes yet again from side to side, like it's earthquake season. Explosions chase each other through the night, like nightmares one after the other. The reporters are panting now. They sound scared as well as exhausted and can no longer tell exactly where the missiles are landing. Darkness is a ghoul. I have an urge to start a fire, burn the whole apartment, just to bring back some light.

How are you supposed to sleep when the sky is flecked with a thousand scintillas of light, when the radio is flooded with waves of static in time with the rhythm of detonations outside? The constant pounding of the warships . . . boom, boom, boom . . . are hollow sounds, mocking the thud of your heart as you lie there listening to them.

A reporter appeals to the ambulances to go to the Zeitoun quarter of the city.

One missile strikes Sheikh Radwan Cemetery. A reporter comments on the strange fate of the corpses interred there—many of whom were killed in previous bombings—finding themselves once more under attack.

The children are now huddled around Hanna on the sofa, staring into the darkness outside.

I feel like a prisoner in the flat as the world collapses around me. It explodes. It cracks. It slides and collapses into rubble. I can't reassure the kids that the next missile won't hit our building. I follow the light of each missile as it homes in on its prey. Each one has an arc, a parabola or a trajectory that you can try to predict. I try to work out each one in the first fraction of a second that I see it. Then I have to stop myself from doing this.

Naeem gets up and walks to the window, before I realize what he's doing. I run and pull him away. Hanna says it is time for the suhoor food. We go to the kitchen amid the darkness and thunder and do our best to prepare the food.

The house phone rings. Sometimes even during the power cut the landlines still work. On the other end, a woman's voice with a strong French accent is expressing solidarity:[2]

"Is this Gaza?"

"Yes."

"Are you Palestinian?"

"Yes."

"I am French. I want to express my support."

"Thank you, I mean . . . Merci."

She seems happy that I know one French word.

"Parlez-vous français?"

"Un peu."

Then she begins a very long sentence in French that I cannot follow at all, but I get the sense of it: the solidarity expressed in passionate words.

I reply: "Merci pour votre solidarité."

"De rien."

Then after a while, the electricity comes on again. The TV flashes into life and I scramble to gather the various parts of the remote control in order to turn down the sound. Before I manage to find all the parts, the electricity goes away again.

The voice of the muezzin in the nearby mosque starts up, singing the call to prayer.

DAY SEVEN

THE CHILDREN HAVE barely slept in days. Nor has anyone. Sometimes a couple of hours just isn't enough, especially when the little sleep you get is stretched thin with anxiety. Worry plays like a lightning storm behind your eyelids whenever you close them. Only when that stops do your hands start to relax. Then, finally, sleep starts to gather around you, slowly, like a gentle whirlwind, circling you and your loved ones.

The pleasure of watching my kids sleep peacefully is no longer possible. Instead, what plays before my eyes are haunting images of the preceding day: a house in the neighborhood struck by a drone; photographs of mayhem posted online by various media; vivid descriptions of destruction from a friend who happened to be an eyewitness. Watching my kids sleep used to be one my greatest pleasures. I don't know how many hours I've wasted watching my nineteen-month-old daughter, Jaffa, sleeping, drifting among the clouds of her dreams. I'd smile at every slightest movement: the occasional twitch of a limb, the faint smile dancing on her lips. This was my favorite moment of the day. But now, looking at my children and thinking they could be dead in a moment's time, that they could be transformed into one of those images on the TV—it's too much.

Instead, over the last few nights, I've wanted to wake my children up. I can't bear them being so quiet. When they're awake, playing, shouting, creating imaginary worlds of their own, they help me deal with my own helplessness. Their noise, the fuss they make, their shouting and running around the flat—all of it makes life a little easier for me. They upstage the sounds of the terrible world outside.

Tonight they will fall asleep quickly, I'm sure of it. The lack of sleep from the night before weighs heavily on them. There's no electricity. The only light to disturb them is the faint glow of my torch as I move around the flat. You can hardly see the face of the person across from you, it's so dark. I close the door to the corridor as quietly as I can. Tonight, I think, they'll drop off quickly.

Back in the living room, I open a window. It's good to feel fresh air on your face. Important to have a break from staring at the ceiling all the time, or from looking directly into the eyes of your loved ones, seeing the fear in them.

My wife, Hanna, and I sit on the blue sofa and stare into the darkness. No light, no details of the world can be seen outside the window. Only blackness and the dark outline of the buildings across the street.

It slowly dawns on us, sitting there, that the rest of the building is completely empty. Hanna is the first to notice it; the people in the flat across the corridor left that morning. Om Noor phoned Hanna that evening, saying she had moved to her father's house in the Rimal quarter. But now Hanna realizes she hasn't heard a sound from the flat above either. Nor has she heard the heels of the lady who lives down the corridor. We start to retrace the events and sounds and movements of the day to reinterpret them. It leads to one conclusion: we are the sole occupants of the building, and the building—our home for the last three-and-a-half years—is not safe.

The gravity of apparent safety is pulling everyone in the Strip closer and closer to the center. We shouldn't be near the border to the east, or the north. We shouldn't be near the beach. We shouldn't be near any government headquarters either. This leaves us with just one option—the already densely overcrowded Jabalia Camp, where my family and Hanna's family both come from. There's no beating Hanna's logic.

People look to anything that makes them feel safer, anything that props up their world a bit longer before the inevitable collapse. Our fates are all in the hands of a drone operator in a military base somewhere just over the Israeli border. The operator looks at Gaza the way an unruly boy looks at the screen of a video game. He presses a button and might destroy an entire street. He might decide to terminate the life of someone walking along the pavement, or he might uproot a tree in an orchard that hasn't yet borne fruit. The operator practices his aim at his own discretion, energized by the trust and power that has been put in his hands by his superiors.

This is how Gaza looks on the computer screen—a thousand images captured by a speeding drone and relayed back to a computer, perhaps a laptop on a desk. The images might include any detail. One of them could be of Hanna and me sitting on the blue sofa in our flat, staring into the darkness. Another might be of our children sleeping in the corridor, spied through the bathroom window at just the right angle. It must be quite entertaining for those soldiers, sitting at their computer screens; it must feel like the best video game ever. I imagine they draw lots to see who has first go.

The drone keeps us company all night long. Its whirring, whirring, whirring, whirring is incessant—as if it wants to remind us it's there, it's not going anywhere. It hangs just a little way above our heads.

We prepare the suhoor. We set the food out in the middle of the living room, in complete darkness. Only night surrounded by more night. I turn the torch on; its weak light fails to hold back very much of the darkness, but it resists nonetheless.

The food is ready. I wake the children and bring them in. We all sit around five dishes: white cheese, hummus, orange jam, yellow cheese, and olives. Darkness eats with us. Fear and anxiety eat with us. The unknown eats with us. The F16 eats with us. The drone, and its operator somewhere out in Israel, eats with us.

Our hands shiver, our eyes stare at the plates on the floor. The dawn prayers leak into the room from a mosque somewhere out in the darkness. Suddenly we remember our hunger, all at once, diving into the delicious, merciful food.

Sunday, 13 July

GUARDING THE DARKNESS

IT'S PAST MIDNIGHT and the shelling from the sea has increased. Explosions are tearing up the beach and many properties along the seafront. Gobs of red fire can be seen spitting out of the warships, traversing over the water, each one carrying its twin reflected in the waves.

I feel each detonation inside my flat, despite being nearly two kilometers from the beach, on the blue sofa near the window on the west-facing side of the apartment. I can see nothing. Only fire. I can hear nothing. Only bombing. This funny blue sofa gives me the perfect vantage point over the darkness. I sit here staring deep into it, and when the light of an explosion flares, I feel it lighting up the whole room around me, bathing me in its light and the sofa's blue. The shape of the lounge, with its two small windows to the east and the west and its large window in the middle, facing south, makes the room feel almost like a chapel in the classic Islamic style. In my chapel, in the middle of the night, I watch the sea to the west—a sea that can be either friend or foe, pacifier or war-maker, loyal or treacherous.

In the midst of this darkness, the radio reporter speaks of an Israeli storming of the beach. They're here.

A few hours ago an F16 killed eighteen members of the Batash* family in the Toufah quarter of Gaza City. Several hours earlier, seven people were killed in Sheikh Radwan.[1] I know in my heart that I live by chance, and that when I die it too will be by chance. How many chances does the future have for you, stashed in its pocket? How many chances have I already used up?

Sitting on my sofa, I feel like a sentry for the darkness; a protector of silence against the oncoming wall of noise, a sentinel defending the unknown from the onslaught of the present. I try to distill meaning from a swirl of unclear thoughts.

Occasionally turning on the TV doesn't help: the body parts; the severed hand lying at the side of the road; the stomach dangling from a limp corpse; the face covered in blood; the skull rent open. . . . The voice of a man from the Abu Namous family cries out; a reporter explains that the head he is carrying is that of his son, the brain is outside the head. . . . The father cries out, begging his boy to wake up to see some toy he has bought him.[2] Poor boy. Poor father. The boy is dead and whatever toy he's talking about is just a mockery now. Destruction. Rubble. Screaming. Torn bodies.

These are the ingredients of nightmares, only they're not nightmares. They are the images being reported from the beach right now. They could just as easily be coming from my street or from my apartment building. The chances are they will soon, but I keep guard over the darkness. I know that there are lights out there, in the world, other than the light of explosions and that there is fire other than the fire of missiles. They might be weak and fading

---

*The eighteen members of the Batash family were Naahed Na'im (forty-one), Baha Majid (twenty-eight), Qusay 'Essam (twelve), Azizah Joseph (fifty-nine), Mohamed 'Essam (seventeen), Ahmed Na'aman (twenty-seven), Yahya Alaa (eighteen), Jalal Majid (twenty-six), Mahmoud Maajed (twenty-two), Marwah Maajid (twenty-five), Majed Sabhi (age unknown), Khalid Maajid (twenty), Ibrahim Maajid (eighteen), Manaar Maajed (thirteen), Amal Hasan (forty-nine), Anas Alaa el-Batash (ten), Qusay Alaa (age unknown), and Zakarieh Alaa (twenty).

lights, from dying batteries or generators running out of fuel, but I have to look for them; what else can I look for?

The sobbing and screaming of children can be heard out on the street; I rush to the window to check what's going on. Hundreds of people—men and women, young and old—are running through the streets below me, fleeing the bombing and the soldiers on the beach. I see a young father dragging his little daughter, who in turn drags some kind of blanket she doesn't want to let go of. An old woman is doing a headcount as the members of her family take a break from the running. One is missing. She shouts "Where is Ahmad? Where is Ahmad?" The family immediately turns around and heads back to look for him, and I lose sight of them in the flood of people coming the other way. These people's houses have been hit by shells; they've seen Israeli troops on the beach.

Whenever you see body parts on the news or hear a radio presenter describe them, you think of those parts of your own body, the hands and legs and arms of your children and loved ones. An expressionless corpse, lungs hanging out of a caved-in chest, a leg severed into three pieces, fingers lying on the ground like scattered sticks, a tongue lolling from a mouth, a heart uprooted from its cavity, body parts of different people mixed up together, lying with flesh they shouldn't be with—as all these images build up, flesh becomes like the wreckage of a house: walls and ceilings, beams and staircases, windows and bits of roofs, all in the wrong places, scattered, amputated, lying on top of one another.

Whenever you hear of a car in the street that's been transformed by a drone into a piece of coal, or see it on the news, you remember that life has given you one more chance. Four young men in a Peugeot—the drone operator decided to put an end to their lives.† All it required was the touch of a button. A touch that takes three young men's lives and leaves the fourth critically ill.

---

†These included Mohammed Walood, Ala' Andelnabi, and Hazim Balousha (ages unknown).

Death is the duck hunter lying in the reeds on the bank of the river. No one sees him; he wears perfect camouflage and picks off each innocent creature unseen.

Whenever you hear the screams of children or think about their fear, the terror that can overwhelm them, the questions in their eyes, the quiver of their lips, the panic in their faces. Whenever you hear the things they say in the heat of confusion, their attempts to understand what's going on. Whenever you consider the periods of heavy silence that hang oppressively over everything you think of—in between the explosions and the whir of the drones, between the chaos of the radio reports and the mortars whizzing through the air. Whenever you remember all these things, and also remember your desire not to remember any of them, you realize that memory is something forced upon you. People do not choose to remember; they are compelled to.

Tonight I am alone in the flat. Hanna has decided to take the children to her father's house at the center of Jabalia Camp. It's safer there, she says. All those who have survived the onslaught on the beach have already fled inland and taken up residence in one of the UNRWA³ schools scattered along the center of the Strip. Within a few hours these schools have transformed from peaceful havens of learning to overcrowded shelters, packed with fear and noise and discomfort. It's an all too instantaneous flashback to the painful scenes of two years ago—the 2012 war—and, before that, the 2008–2009 war. The area where we live, Saftawi, hasn't been under attack so far, but the continuous raids on the neighboring districts eat away at Hanna's sense of calm. She has run out of calm, she said to me earlier.

"One night only," I say.

I tell myself it will be good for the children to leave the flat; they haven't set foot outside it in a week.

I am left alone, to guard the darkness.

THE SCENT
OF SYCAMORE

NOTHING REMINDS ME of home quite like the scent of sycamore.

I never realized this before. On my way back home from the camp tonight I look up—as if for the first time—at the canopy of a great old tree that shades part of al-Bahar Street, and whose trunk is hidden behind a high wall. I must have passed under this tree a thousand times. Whether I knew it or not, its fragrance greeted me every time I entered the district. At night, in the darkness of the power cuts, I must have followed its scent, subconsciously, all the way back to Saftawi. Who knows what this tree has witnessed over the decades—its thick branches, its steadfast trunk. This majestic plant has stood here, resolute, from a time when a small forest stretched all the way from the tents of Jabalia Camp to the sea; a forest I played in as a kid. Now this tree is all that remains of that wood, in a jungle of concrete and overcrowding.

Every night I walk along al-Bahar Street between Saftawi and Jabalia Camp. During the last few nights of bombardment, I must have been the street's only detectable movement. To my left lies the remains of the car that was struck yesterday. At the entrance to my street, there's a huge crater, about eight meters in diameter—the product of the strike last night that cut the power. Glass has fallen from apartment windows on all sides and covers the tarmac. In

Saftawi Square, the statue of a mosque in miniature now lies in fragments in the middle of the road.[1]

Again, tonight, I'm the only person on this street. The branches of the tree watch over me; the fragrance of its leaves follow me, step by step.

As a Gazan, if you're ever lucky enough to leave the Strip and travel north towards Jaffa or northeast towards Jerusalem, you should keep your eyes peeled for sycamore trees. If you see one, you must try to imagine the Palestinian village that once stood around it. My grandmother told me this. The square of a Palestinian village, especially one near the coast, would always be built around a single sycamore—a huge tree that towered over the village like a minaret.

I realize tonight that the sycamore behind the wall on al-Bahar Street is my own personal minaret; it calls to say, "Atef, you're home." Only when the smell of its leaves fills my nostrils do I realize I'm nearly there. Then I relax, my shoulders drop a millimeter or two, my heartbeat slows, and I feel I've survived this walk.

Since the beginning of the war, I have walked the road to and from Jabalia Camp twice a day. At around 5 p.m., two-and-a-half hours before the iftar, I head for the souq, something I have done every Ramadan since I was about six years old. It's a tradition, you see, to send the boys out to the souq to kill the remaining few hours of the fast, preparing for the iftar: buying delicacies to decorate the iftar table—hummus, pickles, falafel, and special Ramadan sweets like *katayef*. This is the easy trip, compared to the journey I make to the camp after the iftar. On the earlier journey there is always something passing by to distract you from your anxieties: a car, a couple of men debating something loudly, a group of boys standing in a doorway. Despite the whir of the drones, the noise of the F16s and the occasional explosion in the distance, these other people on the street make you feel calm about it all. I get back from the souq around seven, my arms piled high with hummus, fresh bread from the bakery, arugula, and countless other ingredients.

My journey after iftar is more complicated. Each time, before I even set foot outside, there's the barrage of objections from Hanna. Each time I explain to her I'll go mad if I don't see others and maintain some normality. She relents but, as I head out, I know that worry will gnaw at her continually until I'm back. I make my way towards the camp in complete darkness, barely seeing a single car on the way, only ambulances or fire engines.

Inside the camp, the atmosphere seems to lighten somehow, despite everything that's happening outside. People are walking in the streets; young men sit on street corners talking. The smell of shisha and the sound of the mosque's prayers fill the air. A few kids can be seen here and there trying to keep the festive spirit of Ramadan alive. Mobile phones have made listening to radio broadcasts easier, so almost everyone you see walking down the street holds their mobile to their ears or has earphones plugged in, listening to the news. It seems people only take these earphones out, and put their phones away, to interpret the news with others.

Camp inhabitants are very professional when it comes to news. They know how to get an update instantly, which reporters to follow, and how to analyze what they say. My first encounter with this was twenty-four years ago, during the first Gulf War, in 1990. I remember all the men from our quarter of the camp would sit in front of the Abu Kamel Shop with a single radio planted on the table between them. Back then there were very few channels to choose from: Saut Israel Radio ("The Voice of Israel"), Sawt al-Arab Radio ("The Voice of the Arabs"), BBC World Service, and Radio Monte Carlo. The men were brilliant at deconstructing what they heard. At that time I was just eighteen and my political education was limited; I barely understood the rhetoric of war and politics. These gatherings outside the Abu Kamel Shop were part of my education, but when I think about them now, I realize that for the men involved, they were merely a process of mentally preparing for the greater unknowns that were always on the horizon for Palestinians. War changes very fast: the technology, the rhetoric, the justifications, the media packaging. These men were keeping up with it at every stage; they were ahead of it almost. It was a skill they had inherited as Palestinians.

Despite the sad history that makes these men such experts, I still enjoy witnessing their debates and being part of them. Tonight, like any other night, I stand with them and listen. When you participate in such gatherings, you have to listen to everyone carefully one at a time. The fact that I have a PhD in politics now doesn't mean a jot to them. Everyone has to have his say. Everyone is frightened, just like me. When an explosion takes place, we all change the channel we're listening to on our mobiles to find the most up-to-the-minute report, to find out where the strike is, exactly. From one reporter to another, war is entering into our evening again—death and dismemberment; screams and sirens. The night is getting on and it's dangerous for me to be out this late. I have to head back.

It's around midnight when I say my farewells. The street is very quiet now, and my anxiety mounts the further down it I walk. In my head, I break the journey into segments, attainable targets, so every block or so I feel like I've achieved something and can focus on the next target. Thus, the first segment is from my father's place to the Jabalia Camp cemetery; the second is from there to Abu Sharikh Square in the Eastern Quarter of the camp, the third takes me to the Civil Defense Unit on al-Bahar Street, the fourth to Saftawi Square, the fifth to my apartment building.

Sometimes, I get distracted and lose track, forgetting which stage of the walk I'm on. On these occasions, my thoughts are invaded by all kinds of speculation. Tonight, it's only the smell of the sycamore between the Civil Defense Unit and Saftawi Square that brings me back to where I am, whispering softly: "Congratulations, Atef, you made it." I look up for the first time to its branches and my fear of drones dissipates. Ahead of me is the square, and behind that high buildings, one of which I live in. I think about the smell of the sycamore consciously for the first time in my life and try to carry the sensation of it all the way into my flat. But the moment I arrive at my apartment door, it's gone. I look back, see the branches in the distance, and I can almost hear the wind rustling its leaves.

Tuesday, 15 July

A CHANGE OF SCHEDULE

NOW THAT HANNA has told me of her decision to remain at her father's house, my entire schedule has changed. I sleep in my flat in al-Saftawi, then spend most of the day in my study, writing my weekly column for *Al-Ayyam*,[1] a Palestinian daily newspaper, and reading drafts for *Seyasat*,[2] the journal I edit. In the afternoon, I head out to Jabalia Camp to spend time with Hanna and the children. I make sure that I have iftar with them, then I visit friends before returning to the flat in the night.

The children are extremely happy about staying at their grandfather's; they can go outside during the day and make friends with other kids from the neighborhood. Also it's a stone's throw from Hawaja Street, which is full of Internet cafés and PlayStation shops—their favorite places in the whole world. Of course, they need to persuade Hanna each time they want to go there that this is a valuable way of spending their time.

The UNRWA schools I pass on the way to Hanna's father's are packed with refugees—or "displaced people," as they're supposed to be referred to. Crowds of people are on foot on every street, trudging slowly towards their new safe haven. From the window of my father-in-law's place, I can see down into one of these schools. These people have only managed to stay alive by abandoning everything they've built up over the years, all their belongings, all their ambitions. My own father's flat has become a shelter for twenty-five people as his siblings, their families, and the family of my great-uncle Abdel Kader have all moved in, fleeing from their homes in Ezbet Abed Rabbo in North Jabalia where so many houses have been flattened.

With these changes, suddenly everything else changes. Now, each day is spent trying to think of hundreds of things at once, trying to calculate or second-guess what might happen in the next few minutes and hours. You have to give up on the long term. Give up on the idea of security or the future.

On the TV, the father of one of the children killed in an attack on the Shuja'iyya quarter[3] on 9 July wails at the corpse of his son: "Forgive me, son, I could not protect you!"* It is very hard to watch, knowing deep down that this might be me in a week's time. Being a father brings with it a deep-seated instinct to protect, but also an assumption that you can protect. You are your children's hero, their superman. You tell yourself you can outwit the planes, the tanks and the warships, to protect them. You can do anything for their sake. But this father on the TV could not have done anything differently to protect his son. Only the pilot had any choice in the matter.

During the 2008–2009 war, my son Mostafa, only six years old at that time, asked me to make the mortars of the warships stop. He told me, confidently, to go out and kill all the Israelis out in the sea. I left the flat and came back five minutes later acting exhausted, as if I'd been fighting with them. I told Mostafa that I'd given them all a good hiding and told them to quit their noise. But only a few minutes later, he pointed in the direction of their renewed thunder. I smiled and told him that these were completely new ships.

---

*The man in question was Eyad Eraif; his two sons were Amer (thirteen) and Mohamed (fifteen).

The attacks continue on all sides. Early this morning, around suhoor time, F16s attacked the Maqosi Towers in al-Nasser district. It felt like the entire city took a step sideways. There were also heavy attacks in Beit Lahia.

The main concern of Gazans is about the land invasion. When is it going to start? So far the war has been limited to air and sea attacks. This has almost become normality as people get back into the familiar habits of survival: how to react if you're on the street in the middle of an air raid; what part of your house to hide in, etc. People's worry now turns to the land invasion: what will the soldiers do to them when they get here? What tactics are there to protect yourself when you're face-to-face with them?

It is very easy to assume this won't happen, to close your eyes and cover your ears and walk among others pretending not to see them, or hear what they're saying. It's easy to pretend you're invisible and to convince yourself that nothing around you has any connection to you, that you're somehow not part of what's happening in Gaza. But you don't have to swim too far out into these kinds of thoughts before you realize the real question is not "How do you relate to the world around you?" but "How does the world relate to you?" Because, at most, you're only ever a tiny detail in this complicated universe. You are only one person, barely a cog in an infinitely complex machine.

In this respect, your personal concerns start to erode; even your gravest fears begin to seem unjustified. What does it matter if you're afraid for your children when all the children in the Strip are in immediate danger? What does it matter if you're worried that your house may be reduced to rubble when thousands are being destroyed up and down the Strip? Is your house any better than these countless others? Are your children any better than the hundreds who have been killed or maimed already?

If I let my beard grow another week, I will look like one of those sheikhs or religious clerics. In the morning when I brush my teeth, I notice white hairs in my beard. I've never had it this long before. It's been two weeks since I last shaved—three days before the war. Hanna asks me each day: "Are you sure you don't want to shave it today?" I explain that I'm reluctant to; I don't want to touch my hair or beard until this war is over. But there are no signs of it ending. I tell her, "I'll see."

A GAME OF FOOTBALL

IN WAR, YOU GROW accustomed to adopting new routines, creating entirely new traditions. An otherwise boring routine in such circumstances can make life bearable. Although death and danger surround you, a simple ritual can help you escape the torment of just sitting and waiting for the unknown to happen. It reassures you.

When you're in this permanent state of ignorance, anxiety clings to every detail of your life: the ticking of the clock, the unexpected knock at the door, the red square at the bottom of the TV screen announcing "Breaking News," the ringing of your mobile, the visit from a neighbor, the ping of your mobile heralding a new SMS message. Amid this whirl of incoming information that unnerves and disorients you, you have to make your own order. You have to keep on top of it, prepare yourself for it as it arrives. You become like a sentry keeping watch on the unknown, hating that which you keep. It's an odd paradox. You have nothing to keep guard on, you realize, but yourself; you stare into your own thoughts and presume your mind to be a microcosm of the trembling, boiling world outside. You set yourself the task of calming this microcosm, imposing order on it, but the chaos that rains down on it is not one of your making.

Instead of living in a labyrinth of the unexpected, you impose repetition, make every day a duplicate of the last. For me, the best

time to assert this order is in the evenings. After the sun sets in
the sea and I've broken the fast, I walk down to the heart of Jabalia
Camp. I visit my friend Wafi's house, where every day I meet the
same three friends sitting in the living room: Faraj, Abu Aseel, and
Wafi—seated in the same chairs they were in the night before. Like
Faraj, I've known Wafi since we were kids. We grew up on the same
street and went to school together. Abu Aseel is the owner of one of
the Internet shops I find myself using a lot.

Wafi's house is small and narrow, too narrow for the patience
of a drone operator to target. Wafi prepares the *nargilah** expertly
and, a few minutes later, brings out juice. The same talk and stories
as last night. Everyone shares his fears and his doubts. And, just
as it did last night, the fears, the opinions, the theories all end up
turning into jokes and comic stories.

After an hour, we all relocate to Faraj's place nearby to watch
the news on his big TV screen. We drink coffee and interpret what's
been said. When there is no electricity, Faraj attaches the house's
wiring to a line from the Internet café and everything carries on
as normal.

These are my rituals. I must keep to them.

At around 11 p.m. I go to see my friend Hussain. If there's
a power cut, he will light candles all around his room. Hussain
grew up in Egypt and is fond of his memories of the country and
anything remotely Egyptian. In his apartment, he brings me Egyptian Ramadan specialties to drink, like jujube† juice, tamarind, or
sobia.‡ Hussain's son has hearing difficulties and he tells me how
his hearing aid was broken when he dropped it trying to escape the
building during a drone attack. Hussain is worried that they won't
be able to find anywhere open to fix it while the war is on. "The boy

---

* Water pipe for smoking shisha tobacco.
† A red or black date, also eaten as a candied dried fruit as a snack.
‡ Coconut with milk.

will spend the whole war seeing panic in other people's eyes but not being able to hear the cause."

Around midnight, I walk back home. A fifteen-minute walk strung with anxiety, illuminated by flashes in the sky, fanfared by the sound of explosions.

It is a simple routine, dull perhaps, but it makes life palatable. It flavors life with that warm comforting taste, just as the spices in Hussain's drinks flavor them. All day I know what I am going to be doing in the evening. I know where I'll be, who I'll be with, what I'll be doing—at every hour of the night. During the day, I await the evening impatiently. I love this boring routine of mine; it makes sense in this senseless war. Boredom has become desirable, you see.

The Israeli army has struck more residential complexes. People are dying in their homes, lying asleep in their beds. In the last ten days, some 630 homes have been destroyed and around 13,550 have been damaged. Thousands of people have been left without a roof above their heads. Many have lost everything, including their loved ones.

Today one of the most brutal crimes of the war took place. Four boys from the Bakir family had been playing football with others on the beach by the Gaza harbor, in front of where they lived.§ The boys went to the beach to play football, as they might on any other day when there wasn't school. A series of missiles from a warship miles out to sea tore their game to shreds. Their blood mixed with the sand and the sea water, while their bodies were retrieved amid screams and continued shelling. One boy was killed instantly; the other three died on their way to hospital.

---

§ The four Bakir boys were Aahed Atef Bakir (ten), Zechariah Aahed Bakir (ten), Mohammed Ramiz Bakir (eleven), and Isma'il Mohammed Bakir (nine). (Jethro Mullen and Ben Wedeman, "'They Went to the Beach to Play': Deaths of 4 Children Add to Growing Toll in Gaza Conflict," CNN, 17 July 17 2014, http://edition.cnn.com/2014/07/17/world/meast/mideast-conflict-children/.)

Elsewhere, in Rafah, a five-month-old baby, Lama al-Satari, was killed when her family's house was struck.[1] A six-year-old boy, Hamza Sari, was also killed.[2] It goes on and on. When I hear such news, I can't stop myself looking at my kids and imagining this happening to them. It might. War doesn't follow any logic. You could escape the worst air raid in the history of Gaza and then, in the middle of celebrating your survival, you could be hit by the tiniest piece of shrapnel. It only takes a fragment. You won't feel it hit you. And if you're lucky, you might be featured in the news for a few seconds.

The news on the TV continues. The percentage of children among the dead is terrifying.

"Dad, is football not allowed in war?" Mostafa asks.

Naeem replies, trying to make sense of it himself: "No, only playing football on the beach is forbidden. Isn't that true, Dad?"

I don't know what's true and what's not anymore. I know that when your children talk about death, you have to change the subject quickly. Think of something totally different that will instantly distract them. But it doesn't always work.

"How come the only sounds outside the house are of drones and explosions?" Mostafa asks. "Where is everyone else?"

"It's bedtime," I say, unable to think of anything else. "It might be over in the morning," I tell them. But I know it won't be.

THE FIRST TRUCE

I WAKE TO the news that Israel has declared a five-hour truce, beginning at 10 a.m. The Palestinian Monetary Authority has also announced that, during these hours, the banks will open so people can receive salaries and withdraw cash.

It's a gentle morning. The movement of the crowds in the street suggests people are happy; they finally have a few hours of normality after ten days of death. You see them heading out in all directions. I take a taxi to Palestine Square[1] and, on the way, the car window presents image after image of devastated buildings in strange black and white—like undeveloped negatives. Great twists of iron protrude from the concrete; chunks of masonry dangle from exposed ceilings, defying gravity, rubble of all kinds covers the ground. Dust clouds hang in the air, like curtains, as we drive into them. I can see blinds flapping in shattered windows above me, letting in what must be a forgiving breeze in this July heat.

A great iron door lies flat in the middle of the road, as if it's just flown there from a nearby building. A satchel lies amid a scatter of books and notebooks, their pages fluttering in the wind like a schoolboy has just dropped them there after a dreaded exam. The street looks like a sculptor's workshop, fragments everywhere, and yet the form of his subject is still deep in the stone, yet to reveal itself.

Houses on both sides of the street are still in the process of collapsing. Their destruction isn't over yet; gravity has still to finish the missiles' work. The dust has a smell to it; it's hard to describe. The sound of women crying and kids screaming drowns out the normal street noises. But I see ahead of us hundreds of cars queuing to get through Jabalia souq, trying to find their way to the south of Gaza City.

Farmers have brought what remains of their produce from the wreckage of their farms. They must have sneaked back onto the fields, after the latest attacks, and picked what they could to bring it here this morning. From my taxi window, I can see the prices on the stalls going down faster than the progress of the traffic jam— clearly the stall holders want to sell every last vegetable by the time the truce ends. I can see the cucumbers, eggplants, and zucchinis are all larger than normal as they've been left on the vine for days. Some farmland reaching up to the northern border has been abandoned completely and all its vegetables left to rot.

When we get to the main street in Jabalia town, it's so crowded my taxi driver simply sighs and turns off the engine. At first I assume it's a funeral procession or a demonstration, the throng is so thick. Then I realize it's just people queuing for the banks and supermarkets—hundreds of them. Also, in amongst them, there's a welfare organization distributing food. It takes my taxi twenty minutes to make its way down this street.

At last, I can see Palestine Square—the largest square in Gaza City and the true heart of the town. To the southeast of this square lies the Shuja'iyya quarter, to the east Toufah, to the southwest Zeitoun, to the northwest Rimal. On Omar al-Mukhtar Street, on the corner of the square, stands the early twentieth-century building that houses the Baladiat Gaza, the Gazan municipality building. I phone my friend Salim and suggest that I meet him at his office as I know Aed is heading there too. From there, we can walk to one of the main banks and catch up while we're queuing. I tell the driver to drop me off at the start of Palestine Square so I can

walk the rest of the way to Salim's office. It's my first chance to see
the city center after ten days of war. Today reminds me of one of
the breaks between the curfews the Israeli army used to impose
during the First Intifada. Jabalia Camp would be in lockdown,
sometimes for months at a time, in that war. The curfews meant
that we couldn't leave the house. But as boys we always found our
own way of disobeying the army. We—my late brother Naeem and
I—used to jump from the roof of our apartment block onto the
next block so that we could play with friends. From rooftop to rooftop we would move along the street—like master criminals, expert
cat burglars—just to spend a few hours playing games with our
mates. It wasn't without risk. Usually the curfew would last ten to
twenty days, then the army would lift it for a few hours and people
would be allowed to go out and buy food from neighboring areas,
like Beit Lahia or Jabalia town.

Whenever the curfew was lifted, the whole camp would be
out on the streets; everyone would be running around, trying to
do twenty jobs at once. People would struggle back to their homes,
laden with as many groceries, bags of flour, and cuts of meat as
they could possibly carry. It was like a free-for-all. The image of
women overloaded with bags and bags of food after three hours of
frenzied shopping outside the camp is one I'll always cherish. One
of them was my mother, Amina. For me, she epitomized the Gazan
spirit: resilience, indefatigability, resourcefulness—the spirit I see
in front of me now in the crush of this first truce, in the people
reclaiming simple details back into their lives, shaking off the dust
of the last ten days and making the most of this island of peace. My
mother and all the women of Gaza deserve a statue to commemo-
rate their sense of survival. There have been statues to soldiers in
Gaza—the Unknown Soldier who used to point north to lost lands
before the statue was bombed in 2005, leaving just a plinth. There
are statues dedicated to martyrs, like the memorial for the martyrs
of the Mavi Marmara[2] on the beach. There are symbolic statues,
like the phoenix in Palestine Square.[3] But there are no statues to

the ordinary women of Gaza, the mothers and grandmothers, who really keep this city going: struggling each day with the rations imposed on their households; fighting with great, heavy bags when they're lucky enough to be able to shop at all; making meager ends meet to keep the family whole. They are heroes as much as anyone else. They should be commemorated in stone.

The horns of the cars, the shouting of the fruit sellers calling out prices, the bray of a donkey dragging a heavy cart behind it, the reproach of a mother telling her boy off for staring at everyone, the heat of July sun, the creaking of old shop doors opening and shutting every second, the constant nervous glances upwards at the sky in fear of a premature end to the truce. . . . This is Gaza on a truce day. My shadow passes over the tarmac effortlessly, the merciless July sun burning my profile into it.

I arrive at Salim's office to find Aed already waiting for me. Salim is one of Gaza's most prominent living poets, as well as a close friend. Aed, on the other hand, works at the Ministry of Culture, having previously studied economics in Poland. The three of us walk to the Cairo-Amman Bank on Omar al-Mukhtar Street and, despite the seemingly endless queue, decide to wait as all of us need cash. After an hour and half, we finally find ourselves in front of the cashier. The young man behind the glass smiles as I greet him; he was a student of mine three years ago.

Afterwards, we walk to Fras souq, the city's biggest market. Everything appears normal, if a little busy. Meat hangs in the butchers' stalls, chickens cluck and flutter loudly in their cages, fruit is piled high. Then suddenly, everyone starts to check their watch. Before too long, it'll be 3 p.m. We have to go. Aed gives us a lift and drives at speed. Our parting words as I step out of the car: "See you next truce."

DREDGING THE WELL

HANNA COMPLAINS ABOUT me spending my nights in Saftawi. She says it's getting dangerous outside of the camp. I want to say everywhere is dangerous right now. But instead I explain that I don't think it's good to leave the apartment unattended. "My point is not about the apartment," she replies. "It's about you."

She's right, of course. I feel more and more stupid each night, walking between the camp and Saftawi with drones whirring above me. Last night, I even saw one: it was glinting in the night sky like a star. If you don't know what to look for, you wouldn't be able to distinguish it from a star. I scanned the sky for about ten minutes as I walked, looking for anything that moved. There are stars and planes up there, of course. But a drone is different, the only light it gives off is reflected so it's harder to see than a star or a plane. It's like a satellite, only it's much closer to the ground and there-fore moves faster. I spotted one as I turned onto al-Bahar Street, then kept my eyes firmly fixed on it. The missiles are easy to see once they're launched—they blaze through the sky blindingly—but keeping my eye on the drone meant I had a second or two more notice than anyone else, should it decide to fire, and that second or two might make all the difference. That was my thinking.

A taxi driver the other day told me that if he drives his car faster than 120kph, a drone's missile cannot catch him. I'm not sure if he's right. For me, shelter is the only solution: run under a doorway, or better still into a building, get some masonry between you and the rocket. At the very least, get under a tree; the branches might absorb the impact.

As I approached the entrance to my street, I congratulated myself on having evaded the drone. Its light had now left the sky completely. But just as I turned the corner, I saw a cluster of new twinkles at the end of my street, a squadron of drones heading towards me. My heart sank.

Hanna's reminder about the risks I take with my nightly walk helps me to make the decision about it. Despite my love of routine, I can't justify it anymore—to myself or to her. I offer a new deal: I will spend the night with them in Jabalia Camp, but will then go to Saftawi to work in my office. The flat shouldn't be left alone. Hanna is a graduate of Arabic literature, so I try a Darwish[1] quote on her:

> *"Why did you leave the horse alone, father?"*
> *"To keep the house company, my son,*
> *Houses die when their inhabitants are gone . . . "*[2]

Since the early hours of the morning, I've watched shells and rockets rain down on Beit Hanoun, to the northeast, and Shuja'iyya, to the southeast. At 8 a.m., the overnight death toll was said to be twenty-three across different parts of the Gaza Strip, although mostly in Beit Hanoun. This number may include the Silawi family whose house, a few streets away from mine, was struck this morning while I was still in my flat—I haven't heard if there were casualties there.

It's now nearly midnight and the death toll for the last twenty-four hours has reached fifty-one. Fifty-one stories. Fifty-one lost pasts and unfulfilled futures.

Tonight the land invasion from the east starts in earnest. The sound of the tanks' mortars introduces a new melody to the cacophony of F16s, drones, and missiles coming in from the sea. A new rhythm has entered the dance. People in the street below my window stop and look up, almost admiringly, at a new type of fire swimming across the sky—tank fire. Much of it is falling to the north. Mainly in al-Attarta and al-Salateen near Beit Lahia. More thunderous explosions shake the building so I step away from the window. I feel as if some cosmic imp is balancing the planet on the tips of its fingers, spinning it, flipping it into the air, occasionally almost dropping it completely, but catching it at the last moment.

I am not a magician, nor do I possess the powers to evade every chance death has of taking me. In any deadly scenario there is always at least one escape route, one way of avoiding it, and you have to commit your whole body and soul to the task of finding it. At times of war, there is always a lot of honeyed rhetoric bandied about, concerning the word "heroism." But it's just rhetoric. The only real heroism is survival, to win the prize that is your own life.

Last night, hundreds of Bedouins were attacked in al-Qaraya al-Badawiya[3] near the northeast border, and also in Attarta in the northernmost corner. Survivors fled their houses, carrying what they could, and walked the dark dusty roads leading to the camp and city, only the whir of the drones to keep them company.

I called my sister Awatif, who lives in Beit Lahia and resolved a week ago to stick it out there, even if all her neighbors left. Her son Mohamed answered her mobile and explained that shells had been falling on all sides, so they left and were now on their way to the camp. I rang them back every five or ten minutes, just for updates on their progress and for my peace of mind. I suggested they stay in my old flat in al-Nasser quarter, which currently sits empty.

But this morning, they announced that they had found a flat to rent in al-Shati' Camp,[4] near their old house from twenty years back.

I didn't sleep well last night for worrying about them. Every attempt to empty my mind failed, as it always does when I try too hard. Then I tried another tactic: to disappear into old memories—decades old—and give my brain the task of reinter-preting them. Dredging these memories for new insights is like plunging a bucket into a very deep, nearly dry well, hoping it will land on its side and will scoop up a mouthful of water from the stones at the bottom when I lift it. This is how I spend my sleepless nights: searching my memory for an event that I can narrate to myself and give new life to; a memory I can resuscitate and pro-long with new details, even if it means blurring fact with fiction. I plunged very deep last night, going very far back to remember a time when I was closest to death, a moment in my life when I should really have died.

The amplified voice of the UNRWA coordinator from the school across the street jolts me back to the present. He is demanding that whoever has parked a motorcycle in the playground needs to get it out, so that the drones don't use it as an excuse to attack the school. Motorcycles are used to transport weapons, the Israelis claim.

After half an hour, the same voice reiterates another UNRWA rule: refugees entering the school must not be seen to be carrying anything heavy with them. "Your belongings might be mistaken for weaponry or rocket fuel," the voice explains.

How can you sleep through this? How can you even think of sleeping? And yet, sleep deprivation will drive you mad in the end: the flares in the sky, the symphony of explosions, the roar of mor-tars, the whir of drones, the voice of the UNRWA man . . . all this chaos will beat you, if you let it.

I go back to the edge of the well, and throw the bucket over the side once more.

I was fifteen when I underwent surgery that saved my life. It was July 1989. I had been throwing stones at Israeli soldiers along with my brother Naeem and hundreds of other boys and young men. The First Intifada against the Israeli occupation had broken out in Jabalia Camp on the very street where I grew up. A year and a half later, it was at its peak. On this particular day, thousands of men and boys had gathered in the center of the camp on al-Trans Street and were throwing stones at the occupying soldiers. I was shot just as I was trying to throw one particular stone, my hand raised high in the air, about to release it. I remember having to drop the thing, angry with disappointment. I was hit but I could still move so, along with my brother, I ran. A soldier followed us for about a kilometer trying to catch up, but he was carrying all kinds of heavy gear. Finally, we managed to lose him. But then I felt my stomach.

Naeem bundled me into someone's car, shouting at the driver to go straight to the hospital. At the time, there were few hospitals in Gaza: al-Shifa in the western part of the city, which is the central Gaza hospital, and the Baptist Hospital[5] or, as we called it, the "British Hospital," as it was built during the British Mandate. This latter one belongs to the Church of Gaza. I arrived barely clinging to life. I remember seeing the faces of my mother, father, and uncles looming above my stretcher like shadows, their voices like echoes of the past. I spent four hours in surgery under the care of an older British surgeon who managed to pluck two fragments of the bullet from my liver. I remember her smiling face and her hands on my forehead when I woke up from the anesthetic. She reassured my mother, who kept ringing frantically every half an hour: "Don't worry, he's going to be all right." I remember her English voice very fondly.

Apparently some of my friends dug a grave for me, they were so convinced I had died.

I recovered after about two months and was able to go home. Whenever my mother took me back for a check-up, she would take me to the same surgeon. The lady would smile and stroke my hair and say in English, "Good boy." Then she would turn to my mother and say the same as before, "He's going to be all right."

I could do with someone telling me now I'm going to be all right.

I was actually shot twice during the First Intifada. On this first occasion, the bullet split into three fragments and became embedded in my liver. The kind-voiced English surgeon managed to get two pieces out but the third is still lodged there. The second time was the following year, May 1990: I was sixteen and again throwing stones at soldiers. This time I was shot in the face—I still have the scar on my left cheek. After that, I was thrown in jail for three months, which I spent in a desert prison called Ansar III, or Ktzi'ot in Hebrew.[6] At the time, it was composed largely of a huddle of tents, surrounded by a perimeter fence, in the middle of the swelteringly hot Negev desert.

My brother Naeem was shot three times in the First Intifada. After he recovered, he joined a militia group, and his name was added to the Israeli army's "wanted" list. In 1992, he was arrested after a clash with the Israeli army in which three of his comrades were killed and he and another were shot. He spent seven years in jail, eventually being released in 1999 after peace talks. When the Second Intifada broke out, he joined a militia once more and was assassinated in 2002.

I often think about how close our starting points were and how easily that could have been me instead.

My mobile rings. It's Fadi, my neighbor in Saftawi, telling me that the army has started firing tear gas now and advising me to close all my windows. I explain that I'm at my father-in-law's place now, in Jabalia Camp. Fadi tells me the tear gas is everywhere in Saftawi now. I hang up and lie back down, and again I'm back in the First Intifada. The army used tear gas all the time when I was a kid. Our mother taught us to always keep an onion in our pockets during army maneuvers; whenever we smelt tear gas we would tear into the onions, rub the oil into our hands, then hold them over our noses.

A BIRTHDAY ON
THE STAIRWELL

LAST NIGHT, at Faraj's place, Wafi, Abu Aseel, and I sat for half an hour or so in almost complete silence. Barely a word passed between us. We all sensed how dangerous things were getting; every minute the danger seems to get closer. When you start to suspect that the next casualty to be mentioned on the news might be you, your behavior begins to get a bit erratic. You flinch at every sound. You mutter things superstitiously under your breath.

The radio presenter listed the names of casualties in full, ordered according to where they lived, and then mentioned the type of missile that killed them. Three boys—a shell devoured them as they slept in their beds in al-Nada Towers.* Three men—at a family gathering in Rafah. Seven members of the Abu Jarad family—killed in their house in Beit Hanoun.† In total, over 300 people have been killed in this war so far, and over 2,200 injured. More than 330 houses have been destroyed, and some 1,200 damaged.

---

* Walaa Abu Ismail Muslim (twelve), Mohammed Abu Muslim (thirteen), and Ahmad Abu Muslim (fourteen).
† Naim Moussa Abu Jarad (twenty-four), Abed Moussa Abu Jarad (thirty), Siham Moussa Abu Jarad (fifteen), Rijaa Alyan Abu Jarad (thirty-one), Ahlam Naim Abu Jarad (thirteen), Hania Abdel Rahman Abu Jarad (three), Samih Naim Abu Jarad (one), and Moussa Abdel Rahman Abu Jarad (age unknown).

Every day, new statistics flood in. New ways of adding up the war, turning it into math. Within every list, there are sub-lists: a list of destroyed buildings, divided into a list of destroyed residences, destroyed offices, destroyed hospitals, destroyed schools, destroyed colleges and university buildings, destroyed farm buildings, destroyed military bases. The losses are measured in agricultural terms, in economic terms, in educational terms, in medical terms. You're under no doubt that the catastrophe is affecting every aspect of life.

Since the early hours of this morning, death has spread its wings over the Strip like never before. I thought I knew wars, but now I'm remembering each one is different. Everything that happens is never quite as it was before.

Ahmad Aziz, who lives in al-Nada Towers in Beit Hanoun, was killed in his apartment at two thirty this morning. Ahmad, who was thirty-four, grew up on the same street as me in Jabalia Camp. We ran down the same alleyways, played on the same street corners. He was killed in his sleep, as were the four members of the al-Zweidi family, fifteen minutes later, when their three-floor residence in Beit Hanoun was targeted. The list goes on. The ghoul of death ran up and down the Strip last night, swallowing everything in its path. Those who escaped it only did so through luck.

During the night, large groups of people fled their houses in al-Qaraya al-Badawiya and al-Nada Towers. They all set off towards Jabalia Camp.[1] It was the same scene in 1948, and again in 1967; men, women, and children walked along the same road, accompanied by the same Red Cross vehicles. The Israelis fired warning strikes to encourage people to leave as fast as possible, so they could then get busy flattening their houses to the ground.

Nael, a friend of mine who was fleeing on foot from his flat near al-Nada Towers, failed to make it to his intended destination: his father's place in the Tel Azaatar area near the camp. Instead he had to make his bed in the UNRWA school with all of the other refugees from al-Nada Towers. In Jabalia Camp alone there are an estimated forty thousand displaced persons.

After iftar today, my father and I visit the Abu Hussain UNRWA School at the northern end of the camp, to see my cousins. Two of my aunts live in Beit Lahia with their families, and all had to abandon their homes yesterday after holding out for as long as they could. Now some twenty of my cousins, and their kids, are taking shelter in this school.

I ask after my aunty Nawal, whose son, Yehia, lost both eyes in the 2012 war. They tell me that she's now moved into her daughter's place in Sheikh Radwan.[2]

My cousins Abed and Moner show me how there is no room for them inside the school, that they must sleep in the playground instead. They have no mattress to sleep on, only sand; no roof above them, only the sky. My father apologizes sincerely that he doesn't have a spare mattress or sheets to give them. He has his own displaced people to deal with at his house—including my sister, Halima, and my father's uncle, Abdel Kader. The most difficult thing is the sense of helplessness; you want to offer a helping hand, but there's nothing you can say or do.

Today is my oldest boy Talal's birthday. He is thirteen. Usually we mark Talal's birthday by going to the beach and spending the entire day there. We would take a picnic of fruit and nuts, soft drinks, and food that Hanna has prepared specially. The children would swim, and fly their kites. This time, I suggest instead buying some meat for a barbecue we can have on my father-in-law's stairwell—it is safe there just before the stairs reach the roof—thus open to the sky but not visible to bombers. We organize it, and we have a kind of celebration. Mostafa teases Talal about the fact that his birthday will be better, as it's in the winter, when the war will have finished.

Let's hope so.

Sunday, 20 July

WHO WILL CONVINCE THEM?

SO I'VE GIVEN up and decided to throw myself on the mercy of the barber. It's too hot to have a beard and the war isn't going to end any day soon. It may never end.

After iftar I go to Abu Annas's place and spend an hour in his son's barbershop, next door. I feel a whole lot fresher when it's done. Sometimes, it's the smallest things that give the most solace. To have a shave after nearly three weeks of discomfort and itching is a blessed relief. It was a silly idea to mark the days of the war in millimeters of hair. You have to take what comfort you can, put yourself before the symbolism. I feel born again! Zohdi is also happy that I'm finally relenting. As my barber, the sight of my long hair over the last week or so has irritated him. Now he clips me with joy. Normal service has resumed for him. When he finishes he sprays some perfume around my face, slaps aftershave on me, and smiles. "Now you are Atef again," he says.

Afterwards, I sit with Abu Annas in front of his house, as we've done a thousand times before. It's only the war that's made this ritual dangerous. We exchange concerns about the situation. Abu Annas asks his other son, Mohamed, to prepare the shisha. But as I start to smoke it Zohdi exclaims that it's too dangerous to smoke shisha in the street. "The drone might interpret the heat signal as a weapon," he explains.

"What weapon? This is shisha!" laughs Abu Annas.

"The drone is blind," says Zohdi. "It's a heat signal—that's all it needs."

Zohdi is right. Neither the drone nor its operator need an excuse to attack a group of people wasting their time trying to forget the war with a shisha pipe. But we should try not to give it an excuse. We have to put ourselves in the shoes of the drone operator; we have to think like a drone operator; we have to respect his blind following of commands, the dumb logic of his mission goals. We need to keep that operator's unquestioning obedience ever present in our minds. Abu Annas and I relocate the conversation indoors.

It's a long night of man-made lightning and man-made earthquakes.

And it's a night of questions too.

Who will convince this generation of Israelis that what they've done this summer is a crime? Who will convince the pilot that this is not a mission for his people, but a mission against it? Who will teach him that life cannot be built on the ruins of other lives? Who will convince the drone operator that the people of Gaza are not characters in a video game? Who will convince him that the buildings he sees on his screen are not graphics, but homes containing living rooms, and kitchens, bathrooms and bedrooms; that there are kids inside, fast asleep; that mobiles hang over their beds; that teddy bears and toy dinosaurs lie on the floor; that posters line the walls? Who will convince him that the orchards his craft flies over in the dark aren't just clusters of pixels? Someone planted those trees, watered them, watched them as they grew. Some of those trees are ancient, in fact, maybe older than the Torah itself, older than the legends and fantasies he read about as a boy.

Who will convince the soldier driving a tank that his vehicle is not a toy? That what he sees from behind his wall of armor plating are not cartoon characters but real people? That the al-Nada Towers are not just stacks of Lego bricks to bring tumbling down on the carpet, but the home of hundreds of real people, civilians, including my friend Ahmed Aziz and his three children, all fast asleep?

Who will convince the navy commander at the helm of that warship we can hear that the families on the beach are not a threat to him; that peanut sellers, or teenagers on motorbikes riding along the harbor wall, are not actually carrying rocket launchers on their shoulders? That the four boys playing football last week are not a threat to the safety of Israel?

Who will convince the international community that it has a responsibility to be objective when things like this happen?

No one, I suspect.

Gaza has no one to help it. The people have only hope and their own resilience to fall back on. If that fails us, the sea may as well rise up and flood the land.

AN INTERVIEW
WITH MYSELF

IT WAS BEIT HANOUN'S turn last night. I phone my friend Hisham, who lives in the Masreen district of the town. Hisham is a clerk in Beit Hanoun Hospital. He tells me the atmosphere there is very tense; mortars are firing in all directions. The street where he lives, which is named after his family, one of the largest families in the town, is a scene of complete desolation. His son broke his leg while escaping a missile attack. It's a difficult conversation. Hisham barely finishes a single sentence; his words die on his tongue, half-finished.

I woke up this morning in a cold sweat, thinking about Hisham and his family. I phone him again and he tells me he knows as much as I do, as he's had to go in to work at the Beit Hanoun Hospital. He and his sons are there, and his wife, daughters, and grandchildren are back at the house. "My wife refuses to leave," he sighs.

I insist that he takes his family to my old flat in al-Nasser quarter; it's not the safest part of the Strip, but it's better than Beit Hanoun. The place is empty at the moment; there's no furniture. But he could borrow a mattress and kitchen things from our flat in Saftawi or from my father or father-in-law. All that matters is that he convinces his wife to leave. The situation in Beit Hanoun is not going to get any better; it stands in the Israelis' way and I know they will bulldoze it in the next few days. A few phone calls later, his wife is finally convinced. Hisham spends three hours arranging the exodus, and gives me blow-by-blow updates via text. One of Hisham's cousins works as an ambulance driver; he will ask the Red Cross for permission to travel to the area, during a moment of calm.

A few hours later, Hisham rings and explains that his cousin drove to the house at high speed and not a moment too soon. Hisham's wife had collapsed from exhaustion and her daughters had to carry her out to the ambulance. They waved white flags for the tanks to see as they carried her. I tell Hisham he can move into my flat in al-Saftawi, and to forget about the al-Nasser one; I will stay permanently in my father-in-law's place now. Eventually, they all arrive—twenty-three people in my small flat: Hisham, his wife, four sons, two daughters-in-law, his daughter, his son-in-law, six grandchildren, his sister and brother-in-law, three nephews, and two nieces. I greet them as they arrive and help them all move in. It's a genuine pleasure to see the relief in their eyes; none of them have slept for thirty-six hours. Finally, they can relax. I show them around, taking my laptop from my office, a few papers, and my wife's handbag, then leave them to rest.

A taxi is waiting outside my flat to take me to the Palestine TV studio in the Tel al-Hawa quarter of Gaza, where I have an interview. When I reach the studio, the floor manager tells me they're running late as they currently don't have a presenter to interview me. It seems all the presenters are exhausted from covering the attacks out in the field round-the-clock. The presenter who was meant to interview me has collapsed after having no sleep for over twenty-four hours. Someone in the studio suggests that I act as presenter as well as guest. Finally, the floor manager succeeds in convincing a reporter based at the nearby al-Shifa Hospital to come to present the program. Eventually, Basher Salman arrives from al-Shifa but insists on taking a shower first and also changing his clothes. He says it doesn't make sense that a reporter out in the field half an hour ago is now in the studio doing a live show. It will all look fake, he says. If he changes his clothes, at least people might believe it.

I wait a further twenty minutes for him to have a shower. In war, there's no such thing as normal. Eventually, he's ready. Before we start, he warns me that he's not going to ask many questions, saying: "Just keep talking, if that's OK?" For forty-five minutes, he basically just sits opposite me, trying not to look exhausted, as I raise rhetorical questions that I then go on to answer. After the program, Salman tells me about the bodies of two children he saw in al-Shifa, from the Kasas family.* They were playing on the rooftop of their building when shrapnel hit them. They were both decapitated. Before I leave the studio, I check the scrolling headline along the bottom of the screens: "Breaking News: Today's Death Toll: 87."

---

* Seven members of the Kasas (also spelled "al-Qassas") family were reported to have been killed on this day: Nasma Iyad (eleven), Israa (eleven), Aya, Aesha Yasser, Lamyaa Iyad, Yasmin, and Arwa al-Qassas (ages unknown).

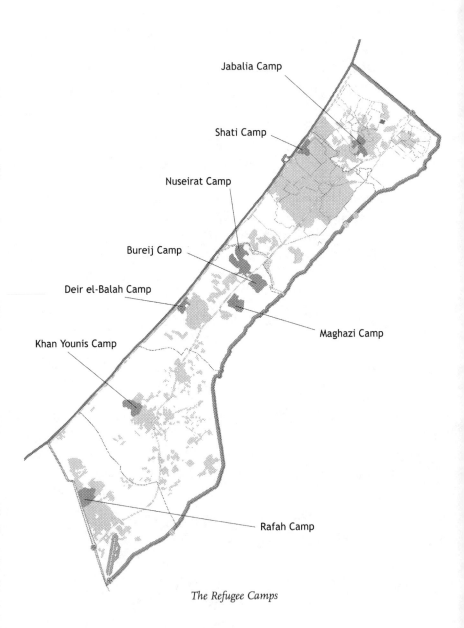

Jabalia Camp

Shati Camp

Nuseirat Camp

Bureij Camp

Deir el-Balah Camp

Maghazi Camp

Khan Younis Camp

Rafah Camp

The Refugee Camps

I DO NOT WANT
TO BE A NUMBER

DESPITE A LONG NIGHT of bombing, I was woken up early this morning at seven thirty by voices coming through the window of my room—newly displaced people taking refuge in the UNRWA school across the street. In the last two weeks, thousands have been forced to leave their homes on the coastal side of Beit Lahia and Beit Hanoun to avoid being killed by a shell from a tank or a warship. They have brought with them little but their desire to survive and have travelled towards the neighborhood I have lived in all my life, Jabalia. Jabalia is itself a refugee camp, established after the 1948 Nakba when thousands were forced to leave their villages and towns across the country that was Palestine. Already the most densely populated camp in the Gaza Strip, Jabalia is now receiving a new wave of refugees after sixty-six years. Some people have suggested this "camp" identity will never go away. The same scenes, same details, same broken dreams, same fears, same cries. Some people argue that the camp will always be a camp. It's never going to transform into something else even if, architecturally, it isn't the sea of tents it began life as, or the shanty town of the '60s and '70s. There may have been developments and investments in the '90s, but the camp remains a camp; the streets are as narrow as a couple of feet wide in places, and the residents are still refugees, whether old or new.

I can hear that the school across the street is now full of people. All the schools of Jabalia Camp have become camps themselves. How ironic—this new influx of vulnerable people. A sense of uncertainty dominates life here—not knowing what you will do in the next few hours, realizing that nothing is certain and that what you plan to do is 100 percent not going to happen.

From my window, which overlooks the school, I can see old women throwing their tiredness down on the little steps in front of the playground, their children clinging to them, many of them crying. Old men are looking nervously up to the sky where drones are still hovering, making a noise that they will not forget through all the years they have left. The UNRWA man is trying to organize everything in this chaos.

Last night was a terrible chapter in the history of Gaza, especially for the eastern part of Beit Hanoun. Tanks moved in from the border towards the residential areas, destroying everything in their way, erasing every building, every school, every orchard. You listen to it all, not knowing whether the next shell will fall on your head, whether you too will be reduced to another number in the news. You think about what it means to disappear from the world, to evaporate like a drop of water, leaving no sign of your existence, and the thought drives you mad.

A shell killed a family of six people three days ago—cousins of my neighbor Eyad. They were sitting around their food, waiting for the prayer to break their fast. The four children were killed instantly and their parents were mortally injured. Eyad, who has spoken with a lisp all his life, tells me that one of the dead girls vanished completely; they found no sign of her body. No bones, no arm, no leg. Nothing that might suggest it belonged to her, that a little girl, nine years old, existed in this place just a few seconds ago. Apparently the rocket hit her body directly.

In two hours, the newcomers are settled in the classrooms and in the tents set up in front of the school. The UNRWA man gives his instructions through his loud-hailer, explaining that everyone needs to follow his orders. The sound of his voice echoes in my head as I try to go back to sleep. You have to sleep when you can in this war, as most nights you will not sleep a wink. You have to gather sleep up as much as you possibly can and store it, as they say in Arabic, "behind the eyes."

Images fly through my head; memories are jostling for position with old songs, old ambitions and hopes. I cannot always distinguish what is a memory and what is hope. My boy, Yasser, is trying to move slowly across the room without making any noise. I see him walking on tiptoes. He doesn't want to wake me up. Smiling, I follow his footsteps. He takes the charger and his iPad. I realize at this moment that the electricity is now back on after a fifteen-hour power cut. My kids are adapting to this war— they fight eagerly every time the power comes on to charge their iPads so they can enjoy playing on them when the power shuts off again. They have their own ideas about how to waste their time during the day.

The first question I ask when I open my eyes is "When is the truce?" Everybody is asking the same question. After sixteen days of attacks, you wish, even harder than at the start, that this is all just a nightmare. Many times I have closed my eyes and thought, "What if I were just sleeping and everything I saw was a dream?" I shake my head and look around. Everything looks real: the tree in the schoolyard moves in the wind; the sun shines; the lady next door sits in front of her house with other old ladies of the neighborhood; everything looks normal. No sign that this is a dream, a nightmare.

Yesterday more than one hundred people were killed in Beit Hanoun and Shuja'iyya. I spend the evening with my friends Faraj, Abu Aseel, and Wafi, at Faraj's place in Jabalia Camp, smoking shisha as I do most nights. Faraj keeps turning the dial on the radio, searching the news, trying to find an announcement that might calm him down. The voice on the radio announces that the total number of people killed during the last two weeks is 567. He starts to break this number down according to where they lived, according to their age, their gender, the method of attack, etc., etc. A few hours ago, a shell decapitated three children. They were carried to the hospital headless. The radio reporter continues his presentation of the situation. The number of people injured has reached over 3,300. Some 670 houses were destroyed and more than 2,000 were damaged.

Everything is turned into numbers. The stories are hidden, disguised, lost behind these numbers. Human beings, souls, bodies—all are converted into numbers. While watching the breaking newsfeed along the bottom of the screen, you can't help but follow these numbers being updated every minute. Before you can take another breath, the death toll changes. Newcomers are added to the list. In the first two hours of this attack, they listed the victim's name and kept it on the screen. Now the victims are just listed as numbers. The names are gone. From time to time, the total figure leaps suddenly—a meteoric leap—and then the news carries on. One of the most frequent questions you hear in the streets is "How many martyrs do we have now?"

Imagine it. Imagine what it must be like to be converted into a number. That you are not "Atef Abu Saif." You are "Victim Number 568." You are merely a digit in a much larger number, one that just keeps on growing. Your entire life is reduced to a number. In a crowd of other numbers, the importance of every number disappears, because what is important is the Big Number. Every time the number increases, the unwritten exclamation mark that accompanies it grows bigger and the unheard screams that accompany each one grow louder. Journalists like catastrophes. They like numbers, statistics, data. They like the sight of tears and emotions in front of the camera. Destruction is a rich meal for the camera. Their camera does not observe the fast of Ramadan; it devours and devours. It is constantly eating new images. Gaza is consummately professional in the production of new material: cooking up new TV food, so tasty and delicious for a carefree audience. Other signs of normal life—of love, of joy, of quiet resilience, of humanity—do not make it to press.

When a human being is made into a number, his or her story disappears. Every number is a tale; every martyr is a tale, a life lost. Or rather, part of that life is lost; the rest tells another tale. The tale after. When a father is killed, or a mother, there are children left behind who are not heroes or supermen, but humans with little but sadness and sorrow to steer them through life; they are children who have lost a father or a mother. There is a tale that is lost and a tale that has yet to begin. The four children who the gunships tore to pieces while playing football on the beach were not the number "FOUR." They were four stories, four lives. The Kawareh family—from Khan Younis, whom the drone decided to prevent from enjoying a meal on the roof of their small building under the moonlight—they were not just "SIX."* They were six infinitely rich, infinitely unknowable stories that came to a stop when a dumb missile fell from a drone and tore their bodies apart. Six novels that Mahfouz, Dickens, or Márquez could not have written satisfactorily. Novels that would have needed a miracle, a genius, to find the structure and poetry they deserved. Instead, they are tales that have cascaded into the news as numbers: moments of lust; onslaughts of pain; days of happiness; dreams that were postponed; looks, glances, feelings, secrets. . . . Every number is a world in itself.

I do not want to be a number, a piece of news, a name on the tongue of a beautiful TV presenter waiting impatiently to finish reading boring news from Gaza. I do not want to be a small number in a large one, a part of the data. I do not want to be an image

---

*The victims of this attack eventually numbered eight: Riad Mohammed Kawareh (fifty), Seraj Ayad Abed al-A'al (eight), Mohammed Ayman Ashour (fifteen), Bakr Mohammed Joudah (twenty-two), Ammar Mohammed Joudah (twenty-six), Hussein Yousef Kawareh (thirteen), Mohammed Ibrahim Kawareh (fifty), and Bassim Salim Kawareh (ten). The surname is spelled "Kevari" in some reports.

among thousands of images that the activists and sympathizers share and post on their Facebook walls, or Twitter accounts, rained down on with likes and comments.

My other neighbor, Ahmad, did not want to be a number when he was killed trying to save his family in the al-Nada Towers. None of the killed or injured wanted it. And nobody will ever ask to hear the stories behind these numbers either. Nobody will uncover the beauty of the lives they led—the beauty that vanishes with every attack, disappears behind this thick, ugly curtain of counting.

Wednesday, 23 July

THIS IS DAY 17

THE CHANCES OF a truce are no better: the same talk every day on the news, same discussions, same waiting. You simply have to wait and see when it will end. Sometimes you have the feeling that it's not going to end. If there is a light at the end of the tunnel, it's online: a pinprick, a flicker, and then you wonder if you saw it at all. Last night, all talks of a truce failed. For seventeen days we've heard the same set of statements, the same questions. Every day is better than the day still to come. This is how it is in Palestine; the past always looks better, sweeter. Because of this, Palestinians are more nostalgic than any other people. For nearly a century, we have lived through a circle of violence, and each year it spirals deeper. We are always the losers. My grandma Aisha never got through a day without succumbing to a lament for her past. Then, immediately after, she would lament for the day that awaited her, tomorrow. The more the war continues, the greater this chorus of laments, the heavier the pain, the greater the loss.

Last evening, my sister-in-law Huda, her son and three daughters had to move to the place where we're staying, in Jabalia Camp. They usually live to the south of Gaza City, in an area called Tel al-Hawa, its southernmost tip. For the last five days, tanks have bombarded the area. In one of these attacks, large chunks of debris from a house nearby flew in through the windows; half of another house is now inside Huda's house! My sister-in-law says they are used to this kind of thing. In every war that I can remember their house has been directly affected. In the 2008–2009 war, half of the house collapsed when a rocket made a direct hit, entering the house horizontally through the lounge window. Her husband, Hatim, has refused to come with her to Jabalia this time. He insists on staying, even though all his neighbors have left. Nobody remains on their street but him. Over the last couple of years, he has developed a passion for keeping birds. He's converted one room in his house into an aviary in which he raises some fifty different kinds of birds, including hummingbirds, pigeons, and sparrows. He prefers to stay and take care of his birds—who else will look after them?

Now there are fourteen of us all living in my father-in-law's house, in Jabalia Camp. The house consists of just two rooms. This morning, there is a long queue for the bathroom. Once inside, you hear nothing but the calls of those queuing, encouraging you to finish as fast as you can. Over the last week, most houses have started to face water shortages.[1] As the electricity only comes on for a few hours a day, and as those few hours are not necessarily the same hours that the water comes, it's usually impossible to pump water back up into the water tanks on the roof of the house. To make matters worse, the water consumption for each house is usually that of several families squeezed into one: of the immediate family and extended families—sisters, brothers, cousins, etc. Most of the people living in the eastern, northern, or coastal sides of Jabalia, or in Beit Hanoun and Beit Lahia, have had to move—under threat of shells and rockets—further into the center of the Strip, to the Jabalia refugee camp itself (already one of its most densely populated areas). My own father spends most of his day watching the level in his water tank, obsessively. The other day, he had to carry water in bottles from the neighbor's tank. He himself is hosting two extra families inside his little house—that of my sister with her twelve family members, and that of his uncle, with his five family members—as well as the family of my brother Ibrahim.

So I'm standing in the queue to use the bathroom—just as I will have to queue to buy bread from the bakery later today. Usually it takes more than one hour to buy anything. I hate the queuing, but I have no choice. Life has to go on. If everyone stopped doing something they hated, the whole wheel of life would stop. The people who seek refuge in the UNRWA school across the street from us have to queue as well, to use the bathroom, or to receive food. Queues are everywhere now. A few days ago, we were living a normal life—waking up at 8 a.m., washing our faces, brushing our teeth, having breakfast, starting our days and whatever our daily routines entailed. Now we have to abandon those routines and live according to each and every moment. We have to improvise new habits amid the chaos. One of those new habits is queuing, queuing for everything. What good would it do to complain? Everyone has to complain internally. The situation is bigger than your inconvenience, it's more urgent than your discomfort. You are asked, like everybody else, to live up to the challenge. You are expected to be a soldier, a trooper, a true son of Palestine, even if you're not, even if it makes you uncomfortable, even though you're just a citizen with no power to be anything more than that.

The refugees' clothes hanging in the windows of the classrooms across the street make me think of tethered birds, dreaming of a chance to fly away, to find more space. To get as far away as possible from the smell of Gaza, the stench of death.

Life is getting complicated. You wish that you were simpler and could accept things more easily. My little girl, Jaffa, was utterly terrified in the first week of the war. We couldn't bring ourselves to explain what the sounds of the explosions were, but she could easily understand the fear written on each of our faces when we heard each one. After a week we started to tell her that these were the sounds of a door being closed quickly by Naeem, her older brother. Jaffa, at nineteen months old, accepted this logic and started to adapt to the situation. She even played with the idea. When hearing each explosion, she now shouts, "The dooooooor!" and then calls out to Naeem to stop slamming it. In Jaffa's logic then, someone is slamming a door to keep us all imprisoned in this situation. Each door slam is a door slammed shut on the opportunity for peace. Each cry from Jaffa to her brother Naeem to stop shutting the door is fruitless.

Yesterday morning, an F16 destroyed a house in this part of the neighborhood. My old friend Naseem Wahaidi—now a British Palestinian—had come over from London just a few days before the attacks started, to see his mother. She kept crying over the phone, wanting to see his new children. Naseem left Gaza to study in London in 1996 and then stayed on, and set up a restaurant in Hammersmith. He took time off work to pay a long-awaited visit to his mother. At nine o'clock in the morning, while everyone was asleep, a rocket destroyed his family's house completely. Large pieces of masonry travelled an impossible distance, colliding with houses at the other end of the street. Some of them hit my father's house. Naseem's mother was killed. The explosion threw her body into the street. His two little girls were injured as well. One of them is currently in the intensive care unit. Naseem himself was injured in his arm and neck. Last night, we gathered to pay a tribute to his mother, this nice old lady on our street, Om Naseem. A few words and thoughts were shared. Afterwards, Naseem explained to me that he had decided to move back to Gaza. He was going to sell his restaurant in Hammersmith and return to Gaza to be with his mother. Now, having seen death, having tasted it, the decision makes no sense to him.

Esa rings at seven thirty this morning to say he has to move from Beit Hanoun. Esa is a friend of my late brother Naeem's; they spent several years together in an Israeli jail. When you receive a phone call during a war, you instantly clutch at your heart. You take what breath you can, before answering. His voice tells me all the neighbors have left or died. He is alone with his wife and they are terrified. He wants to move out. He asks if he can use my flat in the al-Nasser quarter. After an hour, he arrives to pick up the keys.

The flat isn't furnished—everything has been taken—so Esa sends his son to pick up furniture from friends in Jabalia. In their white car, the son moves from house to house, collecting whatever will make their life easier. I manage to provide him with a gas cylinder through another friend, Faraj. By nightfall, Esa is happy—his voice over the phone tells me as much. Finally he is OK, his children are OK. Having seen death on the streets around his house, having touched dead bodies to check for life, having feared all day long that he or his children would be next, he is finally sounding calm. "We made it, Atef!!! We are alive!!!"

It is Day 17. It could be Day 27, or Day 37, or Day 70. No reason to think we are anywhere near the end of the game.

WE WAIT EACH NIGHT FOR DEATH TO KNOCK AT THE DOOR

THE WORST THING is when you realize you no longer understand what's going on. Throughout the night, the tanks, drones, F16s, and warships haven't let up for a single minute. The explosions are constant, always sounding like they're just next door. Sometimes you're convinced that they're in your very room, that you've finally been hit. Then you realize, another miss. My mobile has run out of battery so I'm unable to listen to the news. Instead I lie in the dark and guess what's going on, make up my own analysis.

In time, you start to distinguish between the different types of attack. By far, the easiest distinction you learn to make is between an air attack, a tank attack, and an attack from the sea. The shells coming in from the sea are the largest in size, and the boom they make is much deeper than anything else you hear. It's an all-engulfing, all-encompassing kind of sound; you feel like the ground itself is being swallowed up. Tank rockets, by comparison, give off a much hollower sound. Their explosions leave more of an echo in the air but you don't feel it so much from beneath. In contrast, a rocket dropped from an F16 produces an unmistakable, brilliant white light as well as a long reverberation. A bomb from an F16 makes the whole street dance a little for a good thirty seconds or so. You feel you might have to jump out of the window any minute to escape the building's collapse. Different from all these, though, is the rocket from a drone. This rocket seems to have more personality—it projects a sharp yellow light into the sky. A few seconds before a drone strike, this bright light spreads over the sky as if the rocket is telling us, "It's dinner time, time to feast."

These are just impressions, of course. But impressions are what enable you to process the strange array of details you're given. None of the attributes I'm assigning to these rockets may be true. In reality, I might be exaggerating the differences or imagining them completely. But when you sit each night in your living room, waiting for death to knock at your door or send you a text message, telling you "death's coming in sixty seconds," when you look for your future and see only the unknown, when you are unable to answer the one question your kids need an answer to ("When is it going to end, Dad?"), when you struggle to summon the strength you need each day, just to get through that day . . . in these situations, which are, of course, all the same situation, what else can you do but form "impressions."

Tonight, we spend the whole night, until 5 a.m., surrounded by this orchestra of explosions, trying to make sense of it. At 5:30 a.m., my father-in-law comes in from the mosque and shares the news he's picked up from the people attending the dawn prayer. Five members of the Abu Aytah family were killed while sleeping, just two hours ago.* They had sought safety on the ground floor of their building, thinking that the physics of an F16 rocket would abide by their logic. With no warning, the rocket converted them into fragments. Elsewhere, tanks are now approaching Jabalia, our district, from the east, a region known as Ezbet Abed Rabbo.

---

*Ibrahim Abdallah Abu Aytah (sixty-seven), Mohamad Ibrahim Abu Aytah (thirty-three), Ahmad Ibrahim Abdallah Abu Aytah (thirty), Jamila Salim Abu Aytah (sixty-five), and Adham Ahmad Abu Aytah (eleven).

The war has divided the Strip into portions, separate courses if you like, and the Lord of War is eating them one course at a time, savoring each one. When the war started three weeks ago, back when it was just air strikes, Shuja'iyya became the first course, with more than 120 killed and some 700 injured (a number that changes daily, of course, as more bodies are uncovered, more survivors pulled out of the rubble). After that, the Lord of War decided he fancied a different piece of the Gaza-cake, and moved towards Beit Hanoun. The same sort of massacre took place there, the same sort of mass exodus, only with different human ingredients. Then, three days ago, the focus shifted to Khuza'a, near Khan Younis. Thousands were displaced. Yesterday some fifty people were killed in Khuza'a alone.

Last night, the tanks approached Ezbet Abed Rabbo, which is just one kilometer from where we're staying. Tank shells fell around us all day long. Most of the people have already left their homes over there. In the 2008–2009 war, a famous massacre was committed in Ezbet Abed Rabbo that has since been acknowledged in the UN's Goldstone Report.[1] Everything was destroyed. Not a single house survived the destruction. Corpses remained under the rubble for a week.

The night before last, an F16 rocket struck two streets behind us. War teaches you how to adapt to its logic but it doesn't share its biggest secret, of course: how to survive it. For instance, whenever there's a war on you have to leave your windows half open so the pressure from the blasts doesn't blow them out. To be even safer, you should cover every pane of the window with adhesive tape so that, when it does break, the shards don't fly indoors or fall on people in the street below. It goes without saying you should never sleep anywhere near a window. The best place to sleep, people say, is near the stairs, preferably under them—that part of a building is structurally strongest. The shell that fell two nights ago

landed 150 meters away. The first thing you do in the seconds afterwards, once you've checked on your loved ones, is inspect the
damage. Usually it's just windows and doors. This shell, it turned
out, landed smack in the middle of the Jabalia cemetery. The dead
do not fight wars, by and large, they're too busy being dead, but on
this occasion they were forced to participate in the suffering of the
living. The next morning, dirty, grey bones lay scattered about the
broken gravestones. At the moment of impact, these old corpses
must have flown upwards into the air. I think about this moment.
I wonder what might have happened to the spirits of these corpses
in that split second of flight, what they must have made of the living occupants of Gaza, sitting patiently in their living rooms, pray-
ing for survival.

Yesterday, most of the talk in the street was about this miracle of survival. When everything is destroyed and everyone else is
dead, you become a miracle you don't quite understand. Everyone
is talking about the five-month-old girl who survived a massacre
that took everyone else in her family. This tiny baby was lying in
a cradle. The masonry fell in a pyramid shape around her, protect-
ing her. She made it by sheer chance. Yesterday, six days after the
attack on Shuja'iyya, rescue workers found a man still alive under
the concrete—six days! Another little girl who survived, while her
mother and brothers perished, was asked by a local TV presenter
where her family was. "They've gone to be martyrs," she replied.
She thinks that being a martyr is somewhere you go for a while,
like a holiday. She went on to explain that she's waiting for them to
come back from "martyrdom."

Some people will inevitably call these the miracles of Ramadan. It is believed that, in Ramadan, there is one particular night,
within the last ten days of the month, that is holier than all the
others. It is the night that Gabriel conveyed the Koran to Mohammed. So I can hear my mother-in-law already, insisting all these
incidents are the miracles of that night.

This Ramadan is different though. The spirit of the month has not once been felt. The sense of communion is gone, the fasting feels hollow. All the little details of the month have been drowned out under the cacophony of war. The morning melodies of the musaharati, the family gatherings, the special competitions at the camp's sports club, the night-time telling of stories by the senior women of the household to the rest of the family gathered around the stove. Everything that defines Ramadan is missing.

I've just returned from the souq. It doesn't look much like a souq this morning. Only a few shops and stalls are open, a few uninspiring vegetables. The cucumbers are pale, the tomatoes dry, the potatoes small and slightly putrid; the radishes have long since lost their luster. I spent half an hour trying to find something good in all this. Most of the farmers have abandoned their fields, the vegetables unpicked. The farmers are now all in the UNRWA schools-turned-refugee-centers, along with everyone else. The fields are empty. Only when someone is prepared to sneak back, to risk never coming back, will new produce reach the souq. The prices have risen at every stall, in some cases by as much as 1,000 percent. Then I see something I don't expect: a handful of young mothers are dragging their children, unwillingly, into a clothes shop, as if it's the start of a new school year. Many of the displaced people now living in the schools-turned-camps brought nothing with them so, after ten days of wearing the same dirty clothes, the women have decided to take action: their children will have new clothes. Life must go on.

Friday, 25 July

DATELESS IN GAZA

I ONLY REALIZE it's a Friday when the prayers from the mosque start. In a war, days no longer matter. You don't care if today is a Friday or a Monday, a Saturday or a Tuesday. The name of the day isn't important, nor its whereabouts in the calendar. I discovered this on the fourth day of the war. The war started on the evening of Sunday, 6 July. Most media outlets consider it as having started on Monday morning, 7 July. I remember that first Sunday night in greater detail than any day since, but, as the shelling and bombing continued ceaselessly, day after day, the days of the week became meaningless. In Gaza now, the only thing that matters is the bomb that's going to fall in the next few minutes.

Four days into the war, when I first realized I was dateless, the only fact I could be certain of was how long the war had lasted for. Your life is bound by the terms of this war; everything is tied to its rhythm, its discourse, its sounds and silences. You know exactly which day of the war you're on: today is Day 19.

This morning I decide to go into Gaza City to see the center, visit the places that have been missing from my new routine. As well as realizing it's a Friday, I remember that Ramadan must finally be drawing to a close. A young man is driving a horse and cart carrying mattresses and pillows—which presumably he's plucked from the ruins of his house—in the direction of some shelter, in one of the UNRWA schools, I imagine. The man calls out to another on the street: "What day of Ramadan is it?" "The twenty-seventh," comes his reply. This means that Eid is just three or four days from today. Normally, by this point, we would already be preparing for the celebrations. Every corner of the city would be strung with lights; shops would be open day and night, stuffed with all the latest must-haves—mostly beautiful clothes that we ought to be wearing for Eid. Eid has its own smell and taste; you can't mistake it.

But not this year.

I walk from the Saraya crossroads, heading westwards. In Palestine Square, the Karawan Café, where I have sat almost every morning for the last seventeen years, is closed. The press vans are crowded in front of the Shorouk Tower, waiting for the next explosion to race to for more images. News in Gaza is produced in three buildings: the Shorouk Tower on Omar al-Mukhtar Street, the Shawa-Hosary Tower on al-Wahda Street, and the al-Johara Tower on al-Jala'a Street. It's less than a three-minute walk between each one. Every press agency and broadcaster, local or international, is based in one of these buildings; every broadcast comes directly from one of them. The balcony of the Ranosh Café, situated on the first floor of the Shorouk building, is covered in dust and black soot; the cafe's modest bamboo chairs have sat empty for nineteen days. Sitting on this balcony, which overlooks Omar al-Mukhtar Street, Gaza's main commercial street, gives you a sense of being connected to every thread of the city's activity. Or normally it does. Now, it just reminds me of how much I miss my old routine: walking everywhere freely, from one side of the city to the other, sipping my morning coffee in Karawan Café, taking my evening nargilah in Ranosh, grabbing a falafel from al-Sousi, a little restaurant down the street—queuing for up to twenty minutes to get it sometimes, because the place is so busy. Now, everything is closed. All I can see is debris, collapsed buildings, huge ugly gaps where buildings used to be, ruins. Rubble is the only permanent image I have when I close my eyes.

Women, babies, old men, young boys and girls—all start to move, down in Unknown Soldiers' Square. They're beginning to wake up. A few are still stretched out, asleep on the pieces of cardboard or material they've brought with them—few are lucky enough to have mattresses—which they've spread out over the square's gardens to spend the night on. This was the safest they could do in terms of refuge: the open air. The UNRWA schools, acting as refugee camps across Gaza, have been full for over a week. The horrors these people have seen, the death they've been forced to taste back home, has been enough to make them drop everything and spend the night exposed like this—either in the Unknown Soldier gardens or on the triangle-shaped patch of grass in the middle of Omar al-Mukhtar Street, opposite the Palestinian Legislative Council. These gardens are normally considered glamorous; they are surrounded by expensive shops, the best restaurants, places of leisure on both sides of the street. Now the gardens have become just another refugee camp. As I walk through them, I see that the fountains, at least, are providing a distraction for some of the boys now camped among them—they're making the most of the cold water, stripping off their clothes and reclaiming the fountains as swimming pools, determined to make a little paradise of their own in this hell.

Suddenly an F16 breaks the sound barrier above us, rattling the square with its sonic boom. All necks crane to scan the sky for a glimpse of where the rocket might land. The boys forget their joy and their eyes dart in every direction. I turn and look east, towards Palestine Square. A few seconds later we hear it: the F16 has taken its meal somewhere in the Rimal neighborhood. Like everyone else, I run to the safest possible place: the center of the street. On such occasions, you learn to keep away from any buildings still intact. I run along the center of the street, along with everyone else, towards the ruins of the Issra Tower, which was hit a week ago and in which many families died. This was one of the first tall buildings to be built in Gaza after the peace accords of 1993. Architecturally, it was quite impressive. Now it's just a hill of rubble; no reason for a rocket to strike here.

Once we're confident the plane has gone, we climb down from the rubble. I take a taxi from Palestine Square to Jabalia. In the taxi's passenger seat, a young man splitting the fare explains that, after seeing the destruction of his family's house in Beit Hanoun, his children went to stay with their grandfather in Nuseirat Camp,[1] which is some sixteen kilometers away from where he's staying in Jabalia. Sixteen kilometers is a great distance at a time of war. Missing his children, he had decided this morning to go and visit them. The journey was a considerable risk for him. As he spoke, he explained how his five goats had been killed when his house was destroyed. He bought them six months ago and hadn't yet paid off the loan he took out to buy them. He used to sell their milk, as well as the cheese he made from it. Now they're dead and his main source of income is dead as well. On top of that he still has to pay off the loan.

A fire is raging in a large building at the end of al-Jala'a Street, which connects Gaza City to Jabalia. The Israelis hit it at three o'clock this morning; now it's noon and the fire continues to devour what it can. The explosion has turned the street into a scene from a Second World War movie.

The woman sitting beside me in the taxi, with a little daughter in her lap, says suddenly that she has heard there might be a truce for five days. She's not sure if it's true but she's happy that they're talking about it at least. From that point on, until we arrive in Jabalia, we spend the journey talking about nothing but the possibility of a truce. We are tired, we need to relax. Listening to the news for the latest on these talks is like listening for your lottery number to come up. It's about waiting for that elusive piece of luck. And luck, even in these situations, is not a collective thing; it's personal. You have to keep yourself safe; after all, you have to save your family, until wider public safety comes with the war's end. Everything needs to have a logic to it, even the prospect of death. You want to assert your own choices about when and where it will come or apply your own logic to the chaos. You want to believe that, although you can't escape death, you should at least be able to postpone it. But war shows this up for the farce it is.

Back in Jabalia, Hanna is fighting with the children over whether they should be allowed to go outside. They want to see the street and breathe the outside air. Even when they try to stand at the window to look out over at the refugee-filled school across the street, Hanna snatches them back. My boy, Mostafa, says it's safe today; people are starting to move around in the neighborhood. He wants to go to my father's house to play with his cousins there. "No is no," Hanna insists. They look at me pleadingly. I suggest that I take them with me this evening. What Hanna does not know, and I keep a secret from her, is that when I take the kids to my father's place—which is just a four-minute walk—the kids spend most of their time in the Internet cafés next door, playing computer games.

Every day I quarrel with Hanna about this. In the end, I take the kids for a few hours before bringing them back. Every minute of our walk there we are at risk. Every step we take is another risk. As I hurry towards my father's place, holding their hands, huddling them as close to me as possible on the pavement, I pray the unthinkable doesn't happen.

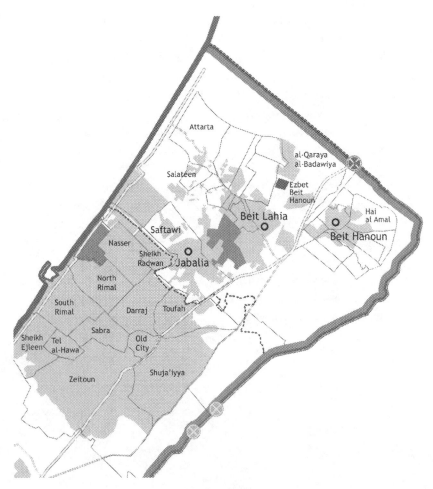

Northern Gaza

Saturday, 26 July

THE TWO-DAY BLACKOUT

IT'S NOW BEEN forty hours with no electricity. The water was also cut off yesterday. Electricity is a constant issue in Gaza. Since the Strip's only power station was bombed in 2008, Gazans have had, at best, twelve hours of electricity a day. These twelve hours could be during the day or while you're fast asleep; it's impossible to predict. Complaining about it gets you nowhere. For three weeks we've barely had two or three hours a day. And right now, we would be happy with just one.

These blackouts affect every part of your life. Your day revolves around that precious moment the power comes back on. You have to make the most of every last second of it. First, you charge every piece of equipment that might have a battery: your mobile, laptop, torches, radios, etc. Second, you try not to use any equipment while it's being charged—to make the most of that charge. Next you have to make some hard decisions about which phone calls to take, which e-mails or messages to reply to. Even when you make a call, you have to stop yourself from straying into any "normal" areas of conversation—they're a waste of battery. Likewise with your laptop; you have to ration every time you turn it on.

Yesterday, I ran out of all means of power. My laptop died, my mobile died. So I spent half the day in an Internet café near my father's place. Having realized a week ago that this war wasn't going to end quickly, the owners of the café set up a large generator and have been open almost 24/7 ever since. In the street where my dad lives in Jabalia Camp—the street I grew up on—there are now five Internet cafés. The clientele in my café are largely children and teenagers. They play games on the computers or use social media. Even now, amid the sounds of the explosions, boys feel the urge to waste their time. Such cafés have a great appeal for them; they need to forget their worries. I'm the only grown-up in this café. I ask its owner to charge both my mobile and laptop. And I sit by one of the computers and check my e-mails quickly, then read the news. I have to wait two hours until my laptop battery says 100 percent. Only then can I face returning to the blackout at home.

Last night my friend Hisham, who works at Beit Hanoun Hospital, phoned to say that the Israelis had bombed the hospital there. Shells struck the X-ray room and the operating theater. Patients, nurses, and doctors—all were terrified. Hisham's three-minute description of the chaos concluded with the insistence that some kind of intervention from the Red Cross or the UN must come. Hundreds of families were camping out in the gardens of the hospital, having nowhere else to go. I phone Palestine TV and tell them that people are trapped in Beit Hanoun Hospital and that they should make a plea to the Red Cross and UN. I give my friend Loay Sadouni, the news editor at the station, the number of the hospital's manager. They phone him immediately. I was at my friend Husain's place at the time with another friend, Abu Aseel, smoking nargilah in the darkness. It was nearly midnight so I headed off towards my place.

There are several UNRWA schools-turned-refugee camps on my way home. I visit the second of them where my friend Ali Kamal, who works as a teacher there, is part of the team taking care of the displaced people. In the administration room, Kamal is wearing a UN bulletproof vest. We sit outside, in front of the school, and he tells me that the school is hosting some 2,450 persons, equating to 430 families. They serve each family one proper meal a day plus a few biscuits. As we talk, I stare at the queue of people on one side, waiting to receive blankets through a window, and at another queue on the other, waiting to receive food. Kamal works a twenty-four-hour shift then goes home for twenty-four hours, before returning to work. Another F16 breaks its sound barrier, throwing a spray of lightning balls across the sky. The jets do this constantly. The preceding explosions reach us from the east from Beit Hanoun.

One of the school's refugees from the Ghabin family went out yesterday during the afternoon to see his house and check on his animals in the field behind it. He was shot by a tank. His family and relatives organized a funeral for him inside the school. Sad faces, bitter eyes, terrible silences all under this metal ceiling, one that used to hang over a sports room where boys played, now a place for tributes and condolences for a young man who went back to his farm to check on his animals.

Women sleep in the classrooms while men find what corners they can—corridors, store rooms, parts of the playground—to put something down to sleep on. I see men sleeping in the playground, under the trees, at the rear of the school. Some classrooms have more than one hundred women sleeping in them. You wonder how anyone manages to live there at all. Whatever privacy people once had gets lost. Everyone shares with everyone else: the same bathrooms, the same eating places, everything. The other day one man insisted that he wanted to see his wife; he missed her. Kamal and the other UN men laughed and asked, "How do you expect to do that?" The man said she was his wife, and he had the right to sit with her, talk to her in private. They explained to him, calmly, that it was not allowed for men to visit the women's room. He did not want to just visit her, he exploded. He could see her in the corridor. He wanted to be intimate with her! It had been three weeks; he was crazed! In the end, Kamal told me they had to let him in, and inside he happily created a kind of tent in one corner of the room, and carefully covered it for privacy. The man then led his wife inside to "discuss family matters."

Before leaving at around 2 a.m., news spreads through the school that there will be a twelve-hour humanitarian truce starting at 8 a.m. It is typical to greet talk of truces and cease-fires with a degree of skepticism. But in the school, everyone is responding to it optimistically; everyone is already planning their return to their homes and farms. In the morning, I guess, we'll see.

The explosions never let up all night long. I have to make my way back to my family to have the suhoor with them. My father managed to buy me a watermelon yesterday. This is the first fresh piece of fruit I have seen since the start of the war. I love to have watermelon for the suhoor; it's full of sugar and water and quenches any thirst. We all tuck into it hungrily. The moment I throw my head on the pillow, a red light travels down through the sky. I close my eyes, hearing the explosion like an echo in a dream. In the morning, the first question I ask when I open my eyes is: Is there a truce? Hanna nods. This time she doesn't mind if the children go to my father's place to play in the Internet café. She is happy that finally, for twelve hours at least, they can move about. She is happy for herself too. For the last hour she has been trying to decide where to go.

I decide to go to see the damage in Shuja'iyya with my friends Aed and Salim.

THE SHUJA'IYYA MASSACRE

LOOKING AT THE rubble where his house had once stood, a man says: "This is not a war. This is the beginning of Doomsday." So much of this neighborhood has been destroyed that, further down the street, another man cannot actually work out which bit of it had been his. The whole street is just rubble: stone, metal, bricks, piles of sand. Large strips of tarmac twist out of the sand, suggesting where the street might have been. But there is no real definition to the street, no limits or boundaries between any of the houses either. The houses once stood there individually, distinct from each other and from the street. Now you can't distinguish anything from anything else.

People's homes now merge and weave together all over Gaza, like threads in a woolen scarf, knitted together by an old woman. Different colors, different materials, different styles. One of the men picking through the chaos starts to scream: "This is sixty years of my family's savings!" This is what I see as I drive with Aed and Salim towards Shuja'iyya. Baghdad Street—one of Shuja'iyya's main thoroughfares, running from the Old City out to al-Karama Street, on the southeast boundary of Gaza City—is the main site of destruction. Baghdad Street, ironically enough, looks not unlike the scenes left behind by the American and British armies in Iraq after the 2003 invasion. Houses no longer have any shape or form. A balcony sits in the middle of the street like a broken chair. It seems to have separated itself from a nearby building. We drive slowly round it. Electricity cables lie severed in the street; trees lean this way and that, uprooted.

A dozen or so cows were killed near a farm on the edge of the neighborhood. Even cows have failed to escape this war. Each one lies on its side, its tongue lolling out of its mouth, its belly starting to inflate with decay. One cow seems to be split cleanly in half. We're delighted, eventually, to see that one cow is still alive. It's standing in a small square of rubble—presumably the remains of what was its barn—and we approach it carefully. It keeps its face close to the one remaining part of a wall. It looks pale and appears to have a leg wound. As we get near it limps away, clearly in pain, but too scared to let us help it. Somebody should tell it we're not Israelis.

Old women sit helplessly in the debris of their homes. A few children can be seen searching for toys. Ambulances and medical teams work through the day to find people still alive under these ruins. Today, some 151 corpses have been found in this rubble. Some of them have started to decay already. You can smell the dead bodies on every corner of Shuja'iyya. One of the corpses found was of a woman who had been carrying both her children, one in each arm, when the tank shell hit her home. It seems she was simply trying to protect them. She held them tight to her chest and, despite the weight of the masonry, she never let go. What they found under all that concrete was like a still life, apparently, a photograph, a perfect composition. Abu Noor, my neighbor, was busy helping to look through the rubble of a building in which six members of a family were killed. The corpse of one child was still missing. Everyone was desperate to find any trace of the body.

Abu Noor finally touches flesh. Something that to him feels like the body of the child. He screams out, calling everyone around him to help him lift the stones. He manages to get a firm hold on a limb and drags it slowly to the surface. It was a leg of a man. Whose leg? Nobody knows.

The truce was meant to be for twelve hours, running from 8 a.m. until 8 p.m. We remained in Shuja'iyya until 4 p.m., moving from one street to the next, trying to process the damage, and help as much as we can in the removal of debris. A man calls us over to the side of the street, as we start to drive east, warning that there are tanks just a few hundred yards away. He says if they see the car, we're the target. We have to turn back.

In Beit Hanoun and Khuza'a, the situation is no better. We hear news that tanks started shooting at people there at 5 p.m., three hours before the truce was supposed to end. In Khuza'a, the car radio tells us people are not allowed to visit the debris of their homes. Everyone in the car looks at their watch to see how much time is left.

We drive back west towards Gaza City's downtown, park up and then walk into the souq near the city's main mosque. The mosque reminds me of medieval churches in Europe. It began life as a church before being converted into a mosque. It has this beautiful combination of Christian and Muslim architecture. The mosque gives shape and character to the narrow souq stretching out in all directions from its front gate. I phone Hanna to ask if we need anything. She asks for cabbage and some parsley. I want to buy some meat and chicken. She asks for one kilo of chicken breasts, no more. We cannot keep meat in the fridge because there's no electricity. So, we have to buy food on a day-by-day basis. In wartime, you do not feel secure if you don't have more than enough food stored in your fridge. You want to buy as much as you can any time you're near a shop. But without electricity, there's no point in stockpiling. It will go off. Once you're back home, sitting patiently amid the bombing and shelling, you become obsessed with how long it will be before you next have a chance to go to the souq and buy more. Everything should have its logic, except for this war; it has a logic you have yet to discover.

Aed drops me near the bakery on al-Nasser Street. I have to queue for forty-five minutes to get bread. Sometimes you need at least a bit of luck or you struggle. Last night, my luck was running low. After forty-five minutes queuing, the man in the bakery said they had all but run out. It was my turn and all he could find were ten small rolls.

For these twelve hours of truce, despite everything—the killing, the destruction, the missing people, the displaced families, the tears, the wounds, the suffering—today, I see Gaza as it used to be. People in their thousands on the street, buying food, moving from one place to another; the shops open, children playing in the streets. It is a city that has poured itself out into a few moments of peace. Now the truce is coming to an end. The tank mortars have started to roar again, filling the air with their terror.

The radio talks about extending the truce for another four hours, that is until midnight. Sometimes you don't care, or you don't believe what the radio says. I take Jaffa to my father's place as my father misses her. She plays with him and then I bring her back as Hanna keeps calling me on the phone, begging me to return. Loay phones from the TV station, asking if they can send a car to take me to its studios for an interview.

In the TV studios, I realize I haven't changed my pullover for a week. The cameraman asks me if this is the same pullover that I was wearing a week ago when they last interviewed me. It is. When I left my flat a week ago, I was wearing the same black trousers, the same stupid blue pullover. I didn't take any other clothes with me when we moved. When I get home I change into one of my father-in-law's galabiya. I need some new clothes.

Monday, 28 July

TODAY IS EID

TODAY IS EID. After a month of fasting, Eid is like a long sigh of relief. The kids get up early, woken by the hymns and chanting from the minarets of all the surrounding mosques, whilst the sun is still struggling to get out of bed in the east. Normally at Eid, the kids play in the streets, excited by the pocket money they've just received from their parents. This is always the single largest amount of money they'll receive all year. They rush out and buy toys, go to the fairground, fly between the heaven and earth. Eid is what every child waits for all the year. It was always a favorite moment for me when I was growing up. It's exactly the same for my kids.

Last night, we all spent about two hours debating what kind of Eid we were going to have. The kids all wanted to celebrate Eid as it should be. This means buying them new clothes, having their hair cut (even if they had it cut a week ago), letting them buy toys and other things to entertain them and permitting them to blow their pocket money on sweets and chocolates or paying for rides. "It's Eid!" they insist. "It's Eid!" That's their logic. Our argument, Hanna's and mine, is that there are many children who lost their parents and cannot celebrate Eid this evening and it is very upsetting for them to see other children celebrating while they cannot. "What about the displaced people camping in the schools," we say, "who don't have anywhere to live anymore, who don't even have the means to wash themselves properly?"

After various excuses and justifications, I realize our arguments are falling on deaf ears. In the end, it's not their fault. They've looked forward to this all year. I succumb to their pressure and agree to buy them one new piece of clothing each, that's all, and maybe a haircut. But no sweets, no toys.

Last night, I spent three hours walking through Jabalia Souq. There was a rumor about an extended truce for another twenty-four hours, starting at 2 p.m. You need to believe some of these rumors just to keep yourself going. But deep inside, your instincts tell you that any truce or cease-fire will ultimately prove to be a joke. You can get a whole range of answers to the question "Will there be a truce?" And each answer falls within what we might call analysis. Any Tom, Dick, or Harry's opinion is an "analysis." Nobody has any real information. People will tell you, "I heard so-and-so saying this and that," or, "I think the situation reveals such and such." The only conclusion you come to is that Gazans no longer care if a truce has been declared or not; they want to have their own truce, even if the pilot of the F16 doesn't want one, or the drone operator sitting at his desk doesn't want one, or the captain of the warship doesn't like the idea of his prey moving freely in the streets. The answer as to whether there'll be a truce tomorrow is no longer relevant. They will have their own truce on Eid. They will enjoy Eid as much as they can. At 3 p.m. yesterday, a house in my father's neighborhood was struck by shrapnel. As it happened, no one was home. Only a neighbor passing down the street at the time was injured. Of course, such information was jumped on by Hanna as a reason against me taking the kids to my father's place last night to let them play in the Internet café next to his house.

Yesterday, the souq had been full of people, mainly buying clothes. A few shops were open, selling sweets and chocolates; it was so packed I could hardly move. When the souq is like this, you find yourself being carried along automatically by the pressing of others. I tried to buy the dried, salty fish you're supposed to have on the morning of Eid. This is the custom. The fish is dried and stuffed with salt months before and on Eid morning, you fry it and cook tomatoes in the oil left over from the fish. After a month of fasting, you need a salty meal to encourage you to start drinking water again frequently. The key to everything is how you cook the fish. That's the secret.

We fry the fish this morning but we have no bread to eat it with. All the bread in the fridge is rotten as there's been no electricity for three days in a row. Only last night, at ten o'clock, did it return for just eighty minutes. This morning, it's back to square one. Everything in the fridge has to be thrown out: meat, chicken, even vegetables. Until last night, the bread was fine, but this morning we have to go hunting for new bread. My father-in-law agrees to set off on his bike to the bakery in the center of the camp. Luckily, it's open and he returns after less than one hour of queuing, laden with warm loaves.

I haven't drunk cold water for three days. Even in the supermarket, you can no longer find cold drinks. The larger supermarkets have their own generators but they don't waste the power on cold drinks. My friend Faraj told me that Wafi brought some ice from relatives living in an area that still has electricity. He gave Faraj some. I asked him if he could spare me some for a glass of water. I feel as if a glass of water with ice is the most precious thing I can own right now.

Tensions erupted in the souq last night. Displaced persons from Beit Hanoun felt the shops selling sweets and chocolates were being insensitive. It was a gesture of indifference towards their suffering, they claimed. Shouts were heard and then fists thrown, right in the middle of the souq, turning everything into a mess. People were divided into two camps, just as the kids and Hanna and I had been, back at home. In the end, I guess life must go on, even at a minimum. No one was badly injured and we managed to separate the aggressors on both sides and get them to explain their position on the matter. The most common greeting we've heard this Eid has been "Thank God Eid arrived while you are still safe." We kept repeating this phrase to the angry people in the souq, to remind them how privileged they were to survive these massacres.

Last night, while standing with my friend Sohail in front of his house, a group of people arrived, helping an exhausted, half-dead old man. Sohail recognized him. He was a friend of his late father. He was the headmaster of a school in Bureij Camp. The Israeli army had arrested him five days ago and kept him near the Erez checkpoint with no food and just one bottle of water. For the past five days, he's been sitting and sleeping on the bare sand. He was in a battlefield, of course, but without enjoying the privileges of someone on a battlefield, namely the right to defend himself from the bullets flying past him or the shells crashing on all sides. A few hours ago, the Israelis asked him to leave the place. He asked, "Where should I go?" "Anywhere—just away from here," they said. He walked for three kilometers until he approached the eastern parts of Jabalia. He collapsed in the street and could not continue. But he had to keep going, to find safety. People gathered around him, splashed water on his face. Finally he opened his eyes. The first question he asked was "Where am I?" They told him that he is in Jabalia. Then he asked them to bring him to Sohail's house.

Once inside, he took a shower and relaxed until his sons arrived after being summoned by Sohail. His story had another twist to it that his sons would tell us. After kidnapping the old father from his house in al-Mughraqa village near the Gaza Wadi, the soldiers locked the mother and two sisters in the bathroom of their house before leaving. The three women were trapped there for two days and nights, living on nothing but water from the tap, screaming all day long and receiving only echoes in return. After two days, someone heard them and broke down the door, finding them on the verge of death, on an edge—neither "protected" nor "protective"—as the Israelis would say.

Two days into the war, a baby girl was born even after her twenty-three-year-old mother had died. This is true. On the way to the hospital, the doctors in the ambulance discovered that the child was alive and that surgery could still save her. And it did. The old man, the survivor, smiled for the first time when he heard this story, realizing that it was still good to be alive.[*]

---

[*] An emergency caesarean was performed on the eight-months-pregnant Shayma al-Sheikh Qanan after she was killed by an Israeli air strike on Deir al-Balah. Tragically, however, on Wednesday, 30 July, the baby daughter, also named Shayma, passed away. ("Palestinian Baby Born After Mother's Death Dies," Alalam News Network, 30 July 2014, http://en.alalam.ir/news/1617749#sthash .lRbMıvXK.dpuf.)

Tuesday, 29 July

DAY 23

FOR THE LAST TWO HOURS, we've heard nothing but sonic booms and the sound of rockets and mortars. Shells have fallen on our street a few hundred yards from the house where we're staying, and on the street behind us. We hear explosions all the time, on all sides, but we're not always sure which explosions are just sonic booms—the sound of F16s breaking the sound barrier—and which are actual strikes. Whichever they are, they continue to force us to live every day in fear of their echoes, fearing that we will become just an echo as well, should one of them turn out to be a direct hit.

Now Hanna is arguing with the kids over what forms of entertainment she's prepared to go out and buy. She suggests simple playing cards and a "snakes and ladders" set. Games that were previously banned are now on the table just to keep them inside. She has forbidden them from going to the grocer's and she's adamant that they won't visit the Internet cafés or the PlayStation shop near my father's place. Their iPads no longer work because irregular surges in electricity have damaged their batteries so they plead with us to take them to a hardware shop to get them fixed. Something they don't understand is the impossibility of normal shopping at a time of war. They have no choice; we will buy them playing cards and a "snakes and ladders" set.

Last night, we all became convinced that the tanks would reach Jabalia Camp soon. All night long, the tanks fired on the eastern side of the camp—the Ezbet Abed Rabbo and Joroun neighbor-hoods. Joroun is just five hundred meters from the center of the camp. The buildings on our street creaked and lurched all night as if about to fall. You feel everything is about to collapse, like the whole city is about to plummet to a great depth. Everything shifts with each strike. It's like you're part of a disaster movie. You're not a lead character in the movie though; you're one of the background figures, the extras, being terrorized or falling prey to the disaster en masse. Your role is simply to engender terror in the viewers, and then to die.

I jump to the window. A funeral is passing in the street below, heading to the cemetery. A corpse covered by a single blanket is being stretchered on the shoulders of a handful of men. Some of the participants are shouting in anger, cursing Israel, the international community, and various Arab governments. The funeral enters the cemetery and the sound of the mourners fades like a cry in a dream. I counted the mourners as they passed—there were fewer than twenty of them. There's a body to bury every minute, right now, and in every corner of the Strip. During the First Intifada, when somebody was killed by the Israeli army, the whole camp would turn out to pay respects. You would be treading on people's toes every step of the way. Thousands and thousands would mourn with you. Now there are so many strikes in the middle of the day, so many drones patrolling the streets, few mourners are prepared to take the risk, even if they knew the departed well. The drone sharpens its teeth every minute, hovering above us.

I can hear the kids fighting over their game of cards—Hanna's plan is working for now.

Last night we all received a recorded message on our mobiles from the Israeli army, warning the people of Jabalia, Beit Lahia, and Beit Hanoun that attacks on their homes were likely and advising people to leave. To where? I wonder. I was sitting with my friends Faraj, Abu Aseel, Wafi, and Mohamad at the time. It was Mohamad's mobile that beeped first to deliver the message, then mine.[1] This was about 9 p.m. We went on with our plans. Abu Aseel suggested that he could prepare dinner at his place, opposite Faraj's place where we were all sitting, and then bring it over. The bombs, shells, and rockets continued to fall nearby, closer than our calm behavior perhaps suggested. There was no electricity, of course, and we followed each explosion with our usual guesses as to where each one had fallen. The radio doesn't help much in this particular game. When the shells are coming thick and fast, as they are tonight, the radio cannot offer anything accurate or useful. The reporters can't keep up with events on the ground and are often in great danger themselves. Abu Aseel brings the food. We eat and smoke nargilah. It is getting close to 10 p.m. before I eventually accept that I must make my way home, and only realize, halfway into my journey, how dangerous it is to be walking the streets. Nobody dares to be out on the street at a time like this. The whole neighborhood has been plunged into darkness and only the flashes from explosions light my way. As I do every night, I head down a street that houses four of the UNRWA schools that are acting as refugee centers. I presume this street is safer than the others. Of course, the Israeli army wouldn't hesitate to attack an UNRWA school; it has hit four of them in the last three weeks, most recently in Beit Hanoun. But in mad times, you develop your own fallible logic for survival. It is not about the safest place. No place is 100 percent safe. It's about following your own logic and being decisive.

Every night, on my way past this school, I indulge a habit of counting all the donkeys tethered to its wall. Tonight there are eighty-three. Of course, I have to be careful to include the little baby donkey that can hardly be more than a few weeks old—one that must have been forced to leave its farm and come here in its first few days of life. The donkeys instinctively huddle close to the wall. A few horses stand among them. Sometimes when they start up, they fill the whole neighborhood with their racket. Gaza is a noisy place at the best of times but now it is a strange, deafening cacophony. What's the difference, you ask yourself, between the sound of the donkeys and the sound of drones? They're both maddening. At least, I guess, the donkeys' noise carries no danger with it. The school's door is locked and I can hear an UNRWA man inside giving instructions through his loud-hailer about best practice. The sound of ambulances surrounds me.

Suddenly, electricity lights up the entire neighborhood. This burst of light can often be a false dawn, but this time it stays. After more than eighty hours, electricity has finally returned to us. Back home, the family has already decided to stay up tonight and use the electricity that they've all missed so much. It is a pleasure for us all to sit around the TV, as a family, and watch something. We don't want to waste one minute of this precious power. Hanna says we shouldn't watch the news or anything related to the war. We need a break. At the beginning of Ramadan she had begun to watch a new drama series. Ramadan is the month of drama for Arab television. On every channel there are scores of different series. She had only been able to follow some of them for a few days. I suggest that it wouldn't make much sense to skip three weeks of a series and then try and pick it up at the season finale—today is the thirtieth and final day of these dramas. But Hanna wants to see what happened to the heroes she got to know at the start.

We manage to watch one of these programs for thirty minutes or so before the explosions make it impossible to follow the dialogue. I suggest turning to a local channel to find out what's happening. Hanna refuses, insisting on sticking with the drama. I tell her there's no point: we have to know what's happening. She says she's fed up with the sight of corpses, blood, body parts, and rubble. Finally, she storms off into another room to watch the rest of it on her own. For me, it's impossible to turn off, to be involved one minute and not the next, like playing in a football match and being substituted off. You want to get straight back on.

There's an influx of newly displaced people coming down the street to the school opposite us. The murmur of their conversations and the cries of their children are audible from my window. They stream past us into the school. These schools are already full, of course. There isn't room for a single new refugee, let alone hundreds. The UNRWA man asks the current occupiers of the school to try their best to make room. Ultimately they have to. The newcomers start to share their stories of displacement, their accounts of mortars and rockets biting great chunks out of their lives, of tanks rolling into their gardens, demolishing their homes and farms, destroying their livelihoods.

I listen to their stories from my window. The light from missile attacks covers the sky. For a moment the whole neighborhood is illuminated. Bombs swim across the sky like tiny, luminous fish.

Hanna suggests that we all sleep in the corridor of the house, near the stairs, as usual. It's safer there. Once the kids are settled they quickly drop off. Then a bomb strikes nearby and they're awake again, terrified. Little Jaffa is screaming. But, amazingly, they fall asleep again very quickly afterwards. Fear steals everything from us, not only our peace of mind and our dignity but also, sometimes, the very energy you need to stay awake. The kids are exhausted by this fear. They lie, shivering in a cold sweat. At least they are asleep. Hanna suggests it is our turn.

I lie awake till past 6 a.m., laying my head down on the pillow in various positions, with no success. The light from bombs comes into the corridor and stares at me. When I try to close my eyes the light still shines through my eyelids. A light that has already shone through flesh and bone and concrete now shines through my eyelids as well. Sometimes I think it's laughing at me, this light. It's pointing directly at me.

Mercifully, it is the sound of Jaffa that wakes me at around 10 a.m.—the sound of a game she's playing on my mobile, a game she plays every morning.

DAY 23: PART 2
6 P.M.

TO SEE DEATH, to touch it with still-living flesh, to smell its saliva, to feel it in your hands, around you, on every corner of the street. To witness its brutality, its vulgarity, its mercilessness. To watch as bodies are scattered about in piles in front of you like discarded exam papers outside a school at the end of term, like old letters torn up by a jilted lover, like the paperwork of a bankrupt businessman piling up at the back of his shop. One leg here, one arm there, an eye, a severed head, fingers, hair, intestines . . . nothing belongs to anything in particular.

To be so close to death.

How death snatches away the beauty of life. How it kidnaps its vitality in one swoop, in one invisible sleight of hand. The ugliness of death is its power over life.

We were having lunch. We had barely started when the ever-nearing tanks began to partake in their own meal—the sound of their mortars thundering through the house.

I jump to the window, convinced that it's just next door. It turns out it's actually seventy meters away and I catch the flash of a second missile just as it lands and watch the first billows of smoke rising above the rooftops. The targeted house is right beside the mosque my father-in-law has just gone to pray in. I run all the way there, forgetting the fact the shelling is still going on. When I get there, the mosque, mysteriously, is closed and appears to be unscathed. Then, along with everyone else on the street, I turn towards the targeted house. The building has been devastated. Men are already busy collecting pieces of flesh that have become separated from the bodies lying all around us. I see everything: scattered organs, severed limbs. I have to pick them up. I touch them. I see how a human can be sliced into pieces like a cow in a butcher's shop. How bodies can become indistinguishable when divided into many parts. We manage to gather five corpses, place them on sheets and carry them to the private cars that have arrived to offer help. The Balata family had all been sheltering in the same room when two rockets put an end to them.

The F16 comes in close again, breaking the sound barrier above us, terrifying us all over again. Several women from the surrounding neighborhood have barely been able to drag their children off the street, after the first attack. Another explosion. It seems the F16 has come back for more, from the same neighborhood. We run like the wind in the fields. There are about a hundred of us. We run down the street, away from the direction of the plane. Death pursues. I start to think I can hear its footsteps behind me or its heartbeat inside me. I look behind as I run. I can see him. I swear to you, I can see him: his pallor washing over the young faces of those running behind me. Then another explosion. There are women running alongside me as well as men, holding onto their clothes and their headscarves as they run, running as fast as the rest of us. The kids are crying, trying to keep up with their mothers. Death has long arms, like a dragon. It can reach out and snatch you on any street or alleyway.

I run into my father-in-law at the end of a narrow street. He is trying to call for more ambulances. I use my phone to call my mother-in-law to reassure her that her husband is safe. The network is busy. Finally ambulances start to arrive. Someone shouts angrily at one of the drivers that they're too late. The driver replies that there are targets all over Jabalia: "We can't respond to every call at the same time!"

We return to the site of the second attack with the ambulance drivers and, once again, offer to help them gather remains from the ruins. One particular ambulance driver seems to be in charge and explains that we should leave the scene and let his team do its work alone. The narrow street leading to the new bomb site needs to be cleared of people so ambulances can get down it. We clear out into the main street but the alleyway is still too narrow for the larger ambulances to fit; only the ambulance car can squeeze through. We help direct what gets allowed in and out of the alleyway and then help with the ferrying of body parts through the alleyway on stretchers.

I open the back and side doors of the ambulance, then return to help carry the stretchers, laden with heaps of torn flesh. Everything merges with everything else. I push my stretcher-load deep inside the ambulance. Death terminates everything. Then I stand aside, waiting for him to end all of it. Hoping for it.

The long black hair of a woman is carried, all in one clump, with part of her head still attached. The hair is matted with blood like the hind of a sheep when it's just been skinned. The remains of her body are like pieces of broken glass, each piece wounds us to pick it up. We carry the remaining stretchers to the ambulance, heave them inside, and then slam the door shut. We do this as quickly as we can but forget that the chief paramedic is sitting ready in the front seat, waiting for our signal. Eventually we remember to slap the side of the vehicle. A sense of relief overwhelms us as the ambulance speeds away, like a criminal fleeing a crime scene. On that stretcher there were two corpses merging into one pile of flesh. Ten people were killed and sixteen were injured in this attack. My whole body was dripping wet, as if I'd just climbed out of the sea.

I return home. Hanna is frightened when she sees the blood stain on my white pullover. She checks me all over to make sure it isn't from some unnoticed injury. I tell her I'm sure it's blood from the bodies we carried. She makes me remove my pullover and starts to wash it immediately. She doesn't want to see a trace of death for a moment longer. The sun is now coming in strong through the living room window. Hanna doesn't want to go up to the roof to dry the pullover there, fearing another drone miscalculation. Instead she spreads the wet pullover over the floor in the living room in front of the window. My white pullover is like a painting of a body lying on the ground, its arms outstretched. The only life in it is given by the sun.

Clouds of thick smoke rise above the eastern edge of the camp, pursued by flames. Strange shapes are cast onto the sky like the shadows of ghosts or dragons, hovering above the camp, waiting, watching.

I take a shower. I wash properly for the first time since the start of the war. I wash every part of my body, every millimeter. I spend longer than I ever have rubbing the foam of the soap into every nook and cranny of my body. I want to wash death clean off me, I want to remove any sign that it might leave on my body. I use every type of soap and shampoo I can find. All five of them. Each time I cover my body from the tips of my toes to the top of my head with soap and then wash it off. Nobody bangs on the door, wanting to use the bathroom. Nobody asks me to finish the longest shower of my life. Nobody complains that this shower might use up the last of the water in the water tank. Everybody, it seems, wants me to wash as hard as I possibly can.

A PIECE OF SHRAPNEL

I SAW THEM WITH MY OWN EYES. Death's footsteps. In the aftermath of feasting on a dozen other lives. His disgusting smell still fills the air. The echo of his roar still rings in my ears. The remnants of his supper still lie scattered around me.

In front of me lies a piece of metal: razor-sharp, a single, twisted edge. It belongs to the rocket that struck an UNRWA school this morning, just a few hours ago, killing dozens. This piece of shrapnel sits beside the school's door. Violent, even in the way it sits there. When I first see it, I flinch as if it's capable of springing back to life, slashing at my face, severing my neck. Carefully, I touch it, then pick it up, start to study its horrifying shape. It may have killed someone on its journey before resting here. It may have travelled through innocent bodies, people trying to rest in the school after hours of fleeing from their devastated homes in Beit Lahia. It may have feasted on their souls and torn at their flesh, passing from body to body before fully quenching its thirst for their blood. I turn it over in my hands. Death still lingers in it, like a djinn hiding quietly somewhere in its heavy metal, like a sleeping volcano ready to erupt at any minute.

Around 5 a.m. tanks hit the Abu Hussain UNRWA School, a few meters away from my father's place.* The rooms in the front half of the school look like they've simply imploded. Five houses opposite the school were destroyed. In the first room of the school, scores of displaced people had been taking shelter—people who had already escaped death in their houses back in Beit Lahia. Without doubt, like all of us last night, they would have been wide awake. Like the rest of us, they would have been sitting there imagining the rocket was about to hit their room. Everyone expects death every night. But he's a visitor who observes no rules, respects no codes of behavior. Hence there's no point in expecting him at any particular time; he'll always be late or early. And the moment you stop thinking about him, he shakes the ground underneath you and destroys the sky above your head.

In the morning, Hanna tells me there's a rumor going around that one of the schools has been hit. She fears our friends from Beit Hanoun have been affected. Mostafa, my second son, thinks it was his school that was hit. He wants to come with me to see his classroom, inspect the damage. I refuse point blank and tell him it's far too dangerous. The last thing in the world I want him to see is the horror I witnessed yesterday. He asks if I can take a photo of his classroom so he can see what's happened to his desk. I agree to this.

As it turns out, the attack was not on Mostafa's school, but on another, a few blocks away. Great hunks of concrete sit scattered around it when I arrive. Dust covers everything and everyone, making the displaced people still inhabiting it look white-haired and ancient. The water tanks that ought to be up on the roof now squat

---

* Sixteen people were killed: Issam Jaber al-Khatib, Said Abu Jalala, Taysir Hamad, Loai al-Firi, Bassem Khaled al-Najjar, Thaer Khaled al-Najjar, Osama Mohammed Sahweel, Bilal Medhat al-Amoudi, Mohammed Moussa Ghaban, Adel Mohammed Abu Qamar, Abdullah Medhat al-Amoudi, Ramadan Khodr Salman, Alaa Khodr Salman, Ali Ahmad Shahin, Rami Barakat, and Medhat al-Amoud. (ages unknown).

in the street. Water pipes dangle down from the walls like figures on a gallows. The mattresses that people had been sleeping on look like great sponges, dyed deep red, soaked. Each mattress could just as well be another body part. The cooking pot, from which these people had been serving their dinner, sits exactly as it was with good food still in it. But no one will eat from it now; those who might have done so have themselves been eaten. The pair of shoes in the corner, the blackboard, the huge tree in front of the school, the clothes hanging out to dry in the playground, the benches under the tree, the faces of the survivors, the noticeboard in the school assembly room, the clay pot in the front room, the blankets, the toilets, the broken tiles, the paintings on the walls of every classroom, the kids' toys—each and every one of these has the imprint of death upon it, a big, dusty footprint. I see it everywhere. In their faces mainly. It is on my face too. I touch it, feel it, taste it—fear that it is not a nightmare, but what I'm really living through.

Part of my extended family has taken refuge in this school. I only remember this fact in the middle of wandering through the damage. Some fifteen people have now passed away, I'm told. I have two aunts who live in the very north of Beit Lahia. Their sons and daughters, and their families in turn, had sought refuge in this particular school. I ask about them. They are not here. I phone my dad and ask if he has news about them. He informs me that the husband of Fathia, my cousin, and her son were injured and have already been hospitalized. They sustained injuries to their arms and legs. A few minutes later, more information arrives. We learn that my cousin Sha'ban has been injured in his back and legs. The rest of the relatives have returned to their homes near the border.

Many of the donkeys brought by the refugees were killed by the strike. Half a dozen lay in the road in front of the school. Their stomachs and intestines hang from their bellies. A seventh donkey is still alive, though critically injured. Nobody does anything to help it. It lies on the side of the road, breathing with great difficulty. Five others have survived though; they stand nearby looking terrified.

Many of the refugees' clothes hang in the windows of the school. The scene reminds me of the famous image of a classic Israeli jail, one where thousands of Palestinians were detained for years, some of them for over three decades. I know it—I was one of them myself once. Now it's the same scene all over again, but here the whole nation is imprisoned. It's an image that haunts those who've now fled their homes to stay alive. It reminds them they are also in a prison, one called Gaza. They must enjoy it, the outside world concludes. They've brought it on themselves. With each refugee center, they've made a new prison—UN-sanctioned prison-within-a-prison. And even there, they're bombed and shelled and murdered.

Diab, my childhood friend, lives across the street from this school. I visit him and find him weeping at the loss of his cousins, killed in the same attack.[†] I knew his cousins; they were our neighbors. A man and his son were also killed. With tears still rolling down his cheeks, Diab takes me to see the three houses of the destroyed family. The fig tree in front of them is painted white with dust. Branches lie on the ground with fruit still on them, mocking us. Diab leads me through to a small room in the main house where he clears a path through scattered children's toys and points to the corner, where they found a two-year-old boy still alive. A little girl elsewhere in the house shouts happily that the big clock on the wall is still intact. This old clock hangs on the wall at the end of a very long, thin living room. The girl's happiness is the only positive moment of the entire day. The rest of the family has been injured. One boy is still hysterical after seeing the flesh of his father and his uncle, mixed together like meat in a butcher's shop. They have yet to calm him down.

---

† Basem al-Najar and Basim al-Najar (ages unknown).

It is now the morning after perhaps the most difficult night of the war. The sky was lit up all night and the shelling never stopped. As usual, it was all so close. As usual, we did not know where each rocket fell exactly. We simply felt its reverberations and guessed where it might be coming from. My head was on the pillow for hours, but sleep never came. We were all lying together in the corridor. Hanna watched the black sky through the window for hours on end. Little Jaffa slept soundly between us for most of it. My eyes followed each bead of light as it fell through the sky. The explosions taunted us. What if a shell had fallen on us right then? We would have been torn to pieces. I looked to my legs, my arms, then to Jaffa and Hanna. Our bodies would have been mixed together. Sometimes you prefer death to endlessly waiting for it. You want it to be over with. You want it to be quick, painless, like a soft breeze, perhaps. If death were a person you could talk to, I would beg him to be gentle and come as softly as he could.

Shells fell around us, closer and closer. An Israeli tank is a blind animal. Death is too. Could this be our last night together? I thought. Jaffa woke up at one point, when the explosions were closest. That was when the school was hit. The light in the sky caught her attention, and she said sleepily, "Papa, light!" and pointed to the sky. She did not know that death was carried in that light.

Now morning is here and everything is different. You see death on the faces of the people in the street. You feel it. This piece of metal—this fragment of a rocket in front of me, which has killed more than fifteen innocent people—reminds me of the light that Jaffa pointed to. It tells me death is still around us, that it is not satisfied yet. It needs more.

Looking at it, I do not want to remember this. I do not want to forget it either.

Thursday, 31 July

MORNING

LAST NIGHT WAS the calmest night since the start of the war. We heard very few bombs and saw only the occasional flash or surveillance balloon in the sky. Relatively speaking, this is good. Except for one enormous, deafening boom at the end of the night, just as the dawn was spreading its light across the sky, nothing was worrying us. Of course, the focus of the onslaught might have moved to other areas of the Strip, Rafah perhaps; it could be just as bad as ever there or in other regions. Whatever the truth, we slept like we hadn't slept in a month. The electricity came on just before 11 p.m. so we had the pleasure of watching TV for a few hours. And, deciding that no news should be heard in our house for a change, we watched a movie then all fell asleep together. Contrary to what we'd grown to expect, we slept soundly for hours. We had started the night scared, as always, imagining the shells hitting us directly, cutting us all to shreds.

When I wake up, I don't want to listen to the radio or phone a friend to ask about the latest developments. I want the morning to be like a normal morning, before the war. To start my day with a cup of coffee, to sip it in private for an hour. To look down from my window and watch the people in the street, to feel the pulse of the camp around me.

I suggest to Hanna that we have a proper breakfast—hummus, *ful*, falafel. But after an hour of visiting all the restaurants in the neighborhood, my son Mostafa returns with the news that falafel can no longer be bought in Jabalia Camp. My father-in-law explains that this might be because falafel requires a lot of boiled oil, which in turn requires lots of gas. As there is still no clue when the war might end, everyone is saving every gas cylinder they have. Hanna suggests the lack of parsley in the market might be another cause; parsley is essential for making good falafel. The family conversation turns to the peculiarities of making falafel. A very simple food—which you can normally find on every street in Gaza and that most Gazan families have every day for breakfast, the cheapest meal imaginable—has turned out to be more complicated.

My mother-in-law is watering her plants despite the shortage of water in the tanks. She keeps her plants in the living room in different pots arranged around the room. They make the house calmer, greener. There are some thirteen different plants in total—they make up her garden. Every morning she waters them and checks each leaf, remembers each one, and notices whenever a new leaf buds into life. She knows their length and their sheen. She knows if they're thirsty from the colors of their leaves. She always finds water for them.

A minute later she is complaining that my eldest boy, Talal, is taking too much time in the shower. She finishes watering her plants and starts shouting at Talal to finish. From behind the door, he explains that he has only just started. She asks him to get out. It is enough to spend five minutes under the shower. At this very moment, her plants are appreciating the water soaking into the soil around their roots.

I shave. The bathroom is very dark. The light coming from the little window is too feeble for me to see properly. I turn on the torch, and start shaving one-handed, shining the torch at my jaw with the other hand. A Gaza TV journalist phones, making sure I will be ready in thirty minutes' time; they're going to send me a taxi. After ten minutes, he calls to apologize that the taxi rank has refused to send taxis to Jabalia. They're afraid their cars will be hit since Jabalia is now a no-go zone.

I phone Aed to ask about this. He is none the wiser. He says he too passed a calm night and slept well. Aed has moved from his place on the north beach to his sister's house in the al-Nasser quarter of Gaza City. He asks me about Berri. Berri is the waiter at the Karawan Café. He is the most famous café waiter in Gaza. He is the best. "Is it open?" he asks about the café. We decide to meet at 11:30 a.m. on the Saraya crossroads and go from there. If not we will look for another place to spend the morning. We have to recapture some normality, to reclaim some of the life we had before. The Karawan Café is a very important ingredient of this normality. As soon as we find a seat, the same old question returns: will there be a truce?

EVENING

I meet Aed and suggest we try to find a restaurant somewhere that's still serving falafel. But everywhere seems closed. Eventually we try one called Akila, on al-Wahda Street. It's open and we both tuck in joyfully. Afterwards we drive through the Old City, and try to take in the destruction on all sides. Broken glass seems to cover every square foot of the town. Rubble is practically the only image your eyes process. Few cars pass. Shops remain closed; they might open when there's a truce. The city operates according to the rhythm of the war. It sets its clock by it. Many buildings have completely disappeared, as if a designer somewhere had simply Photoshopped them out of the picture—the designer being an F16 pilot, a drone operator, a soldier sitting in a warship or a tank. Each designer competes for a turn to delete the next part of the photograph. Seated in front of screens, far, far away from where their killing machines have their effect, they each take turns playing their favorite game. In many streets, more than one building has been deleted. Some buildings have had only one side deleted, or a top floor, or patches of wall. Someone has been busy at his desk, clicking and dragging, erasing and erasing. So busy in fact that, if I come tomorrow, I will barely recognize the street again; the photograph will have changed so much, the game moved on.

Unfortunately, Karawan Café is closed, Ranosh likewise. There is no place to have nargilah. Aed suggests that we get cold drinks and ice cream and go to our friend Salim's house nearby. I haven't tasted cold water for several days, or any cold drink. Finally, I find a shop, near Salim's, where I can buy two bottles of cold water and two Cokes. The building opposite Salim's has been destroyed. He hasn't had water himself for two days. When we arrive he is working with other inhabitants in the building to fix the usual problem. Naturally Salim's building doesn't have electricity, however the building at the end of the street has its own generator. Salim and his neighbors have persuaded the occupants of that building to run a line to theirs, just for a couple of hours, so they can pump water up to the tanks. But their attempts have so far failed as the line doesn't seem to be connecting properly or has some kind of break in it. Salim's seventy-year-old mother is fretting that the problem will never be fixed. It isn't until 8 p.m. that the current is connected.

We eat ice cream, drink the Coke, and smoke shisha, listening to the sound of the tank slowly filling. We chat for a couple of hours, then leave Salim thinking about how to ration the water when the tank is full. On my way back, I see people queuing in the hundreds to buy bread. Then the bombing starts again and I rush back to Jabalia. Hanna has been back to our flat in Saftawi to gather fresh clothes. The moment she arrived, she tells me, an F16 struck the block next door—one surrounded by a small, beautiful orange orchard—destroying it.

Friday, 1 August

THE LOGIC OF
DISTRIBUTION

THE SOUND OF THE UNRWA organizer's long list of instructions, read through a loud-hailer, filters into the house from the school across the road. At this time every morning, all the displaced people taking refuge in the school have to listen carefully. They have assembled in groups in front of the building. The remnants of sleep can still be seen on their faces. A few kids are crying, rubbing their eyes. It's obvious, even from my window, that they're being forced to listen to these instructions against their will. Everyone has to pay complete attention. It is the same obligation to attentiveness that also woke me up, hearing each and every rule and protocol crystal clear, despite my sore throat.

The UNRWA man tells everyone that a three-day truce has been declared, starting this morning, and the hope is, it will become a permanent truce. He is not clear whether people should, or can, go back to their homes. The decision is theirs; it is ultimately their responsibility. In other words, UNRWA is not actively encouraging people to return just yet, but they may if they choose. The school will continue to provide shelter to the people registered as displaced, until it is deemed completely safe.

"A three-day truce! A three-day truce . . . !"

This is big news.

People start to exchange opinions on the situation. Despite their disappointment with it only being for three days, they're glad to be able to relax finally and breathe a little more easily. Most of these displaced people decide to go back to see their homes, to enjoy some proper rest and, most importantly, privacy.

My kids are arguing with their mother about the usual: permission to play with their friends in the PlayStation shop near their grandfather's house. In their eyes, there is no point in worrying. They know the arguments their mother will put up against them going: "What if the truce is broken suddenly while they are out playing?" That sort of thing. This is one of the happiest moments of the last month, they say. Everyone is relaxed. The truce is longer than anyone even contemplated, and people are starting to do all kinds of things once more.

The TV talks of Palestinian representatives who have travelled to Cairo to negotiate the conditions of the cease-fire with the Egyptian government.[1] My mother-in-law asks me, "Do you think they'll come to an agreement?" "I hope so," I reply. She is not happy with my answer. She needs a definite answer. From her face and the way she pronounces the words, she seems unsure if they are ever going to agree. Ultimately, she concludes, the war must end soon, before it becomes normal, before it becomes a permanent component of our daily discourse. When she hears the sound of the door closing behind the kids, she asks Hanna if she is sure it's safe for them to go. Hanna is not convinced, I know, but says "Of course! Of course!"

From the window of the living room, I see hordes of people leaving the UNRWA school opposite, heading north, west, and east back towards their homes. Some have selected to stay, to "wait and see." Many families have decided to divide in two; one half going home to see if things are safe, to check on the house or the farm, the other half (including the children, of course) remaining in the school, should the first half never come back.

It's the same logic my friend Faraj is using when he distributes his family every night among different rooms of the house.

This family of seven people sleeps in three different rooms. If a shell lands on one room, other members of the family will survive. This is just one example of the madness that informs your every decision. You strategize not only your own survival, but your whole extended family's. Yesterday, a farmer from the Sheikh Ejleen area, south of Gaza City, explained to me how he sneaks with his family back to the farm each morning, at 6 a.m., to pick cucumbers, tomatoes, figs, and grapes. The farmland is right beside the beach and they work the fields in the early hours whilst the warships send missiles over their heads towards the city. The grapes you get from Sheikh Ejleen are the best grapes you're ever likely to taste. The farmer explains that this is his livelihood; he has no choice but to protect it and keep it going.

Last night was one of the most violent of the war so far. Shells and rockets fell all through the small hours. Each night, we become convinced the explosions are getting closer and closer, even if our rational brain knows they can't always be. One of the rhythms of this war we've grown used to is that truces, or attempted truces, are usually preceded by particularly bad nights. So it was a prerequisite that last night would be bad—being the eve of a three-day cease-fire. In the same vein, if things are calm you know they will only get worse. This is another example of the strange logic of war; there's no sense to it, but there is a kind of absurd logic. You cling to it, especially in the hardest moments—like last night. The Israeli killing machine was eating as much as it could before it fasted. It was filling its stomach.

It's now 2 p.m. and my father-in-law is telling me the truce has just broken down. Some forty people have been killed in Rafah. Hanna phones the boys, Talal and Mostafa, on their mobiles, asking them to return immediately.

"But the truce!" they argue.

"There is no truce."

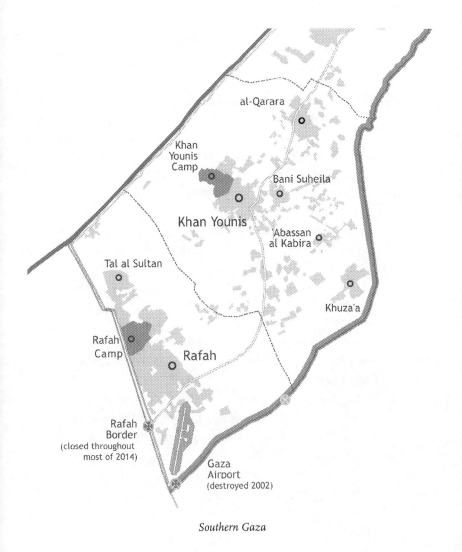

al-Qarara

Khan
Younis
Camp

Bani Suheila

Khan Younis

Abassan
al Kabira

Tal al Sultan

Khuza'a

Rafah
Camp

Rafah

Rafah
Border
(closed throughout
most of 2014)

Gaza
Airport
(destroyed 2002)

Southern Gaza

Saturday, 2 August

DEATH IN RAFAH

MY THROAT HAS GROWN WORSE. It's excruciatingly dry and has been joined by a pain in my chest and a weakness all over my body. When the sore throat started, Sharif, the pharmacist, told me it was probably sensitivity to all the concrete dust and smoke hanging in the city air. Last night, I was at my friend Wafi's place, exchanging opinions and speculations into the early hours. In the middle of the conversation, Abu Aseel confirmed my worst fears. Hanna had told me earlier in the day that, at around 2 a.m. the previous morning, a thick plume of low-lying white smoke had been seen encroaching on the camp from the east. It had made her cough all day. Now Abu Aseel was explaining that he was out in the street when the cloud reached him: "I could barely see my hands in front of me." He was also suffering from chest and throat pains. Wafi had smelled it too and had been coughing all day. They all agreed it was probably poison gas. Apparently, everybody saw and smelt it except me. I hadn't slept well that night so it was strange that I hadn't noticed it. Hanna said that I coughed during the night too, but I was only half awake.

Sharif is the owner of the Balsam Pharmacy. It is the oldest pharmacy in the camp, a business he inherited from his father. When I asked him two days ago he assured me that my sore throat was normal given the amount of dust in the air and told me not to worry, that in two days the pain would be gone. Hanna passed his pharmacy yesterday afternoon and informed him that my pain was still as bad as ever. He gave her more medicine, which he promised would fix it. Yesterday morning, I could barely get out of bed, I felt so weak. So Hanna gave me the medicine in bed. Only at 3 p.m. did I eventually get up and have something to eat.

My father-in-law informs me that the Israeli army might withdraw from one side of Beit Lahia tonight. I had felt so sick during the night that I wasn't aware what was happening. This is one of the miracles of falling sick in the time of war. Sleeping soundly and not noticing or caring about the world as it falls apart around you. That was how I passed last night, in pain but carefree. I didn't seem to hear the explosions or notice the lights in the sky. I didn't care if a rocket made a direct hit and tore my body to pieces. I just closed my eyes and slept. I almost wish I could remain this sick throughout the war—detached from the disaster surrounding me. Unplugged, disconnected.

But this afternoon I feel a bit more human. So there's lots of news to catch up on.

My mother-in-law starts by lamenting the misfortune of her nieces who had to spend their night on the street because the drones attacked their home. After the first rocket fell in the middle of the night, they fled into the street. They were lucky to be already awake when the first one struck otherwise they would not have been able to move fast enough to avoid the second, which hit the room they were in. They picked up their children and ran. Now my mother-in-law's brother is hosting six families at his place, a total guest list of over one hundred! His house is beginning to resemble one of the UNRWA schools.

The main mosque in the center of the camp was hit as well. The muezzin's call to prayers can no longer be heard. He fled in case a second rocket followed. So far, it hasn't fallen yet. People avoid walking anywhere near the mosque now. In the old days, this was the only mosque in the camp. When I was a child, I would pray there. It means many things to me; it's central to my childhood memories and the person I was.

More than a hundred were killed in Rafah last night. This simple border town, which has been quiet for most of the war, has suddenly become the center of a new wave of attacks. Israel has accused Palestinian militia there of capturing a soldier after a battle in which two other Israeli soldiers were killed. The Palestinians denied these accusations so Israel broke the three-day truce and declared a whole new war on Rafah until the soldier is found. In one attack, some forty civilians were killed. The people of Rafah are not allowed to leave their homes. Israel has been using local radio channels, hacking into the wavelength, to deliver its messages to Gazans. In the middle of listening to music at my friend Wafi's house, we hear the broadcast cut short suddenly and the voice of an Israeli general, threatening the people of Rafah. Any person walking in the street, any person driving a car will be hit. After the wavelength is given back to the station, we hear a flurry of new reports, including the head of the hospital in Rafah explaining that the Israeli army told them to evacuate the hospital immediately and to carry all the sick and injured into the street (even though they were also threatening to hit people in the street). "A humanitarian crisis is approaching, and it will be on your head!" the voice on the phone said to him.

I can hear the sound of my kids playing cards with their grandmother in the next room. She has not felt calm for over a month. Nobody fears war more than her. And yet she always manages to keep her composure. She is enjoying playing with the children. Only the sound of little Jaffa crying makes the scene a little incomplete.

It would seem that I have acquired a new job title: administrator of the Internet café. I spend more than an hour a day using the main administrative computer in the café next to my father's house. Power shortages at home are old news—it comes on randomly for an hour a day, sometimes not at all for four days, sometimes only for an hour in the middle of the night. Because of this, I have taken up almost permanent residence in the Internet café, which has its own generator. Each day I spend hours there, checking my e-mails, writing and filing my copy, and then, if there's time, reading newspapers online. The manager of the café is very understanding and lets me use his main computer. In return I have to organize his online timetable for the use of other computers in the café. For one shekel, customers can be online for thirty-five minutes. I have to go to the prepaid box and add their time. Some people prefer an open-ended slot. I simply need to double-click on the box that identifies that particular computer. I acquire new skills all the time. Customers shout out their requests to start or terminate a session from the front of the café and I click the appropriate box then carry on with my work. I have become an Internet-café boy! I like it, in fact; at least it enables me to do my work. I have the café's opening times etched on my brain. The whole neighborhood seems to turn up at some point in the day to charge their laptops, mobiles, and torches.

Now more news is coming over the airwaves on my father-in-law's radio. Israel is declaring that it has decided to complete its operation in Gaza. I'm not sure what to make of this. In Gaza you learn not to trust anything. Hanna says the first thing she wants to do when the war finally finishes is go to see the damage in Beit Hanoun and Shuja'iyya. The kids are screaming they want their iPads fixed. I want to breathe clean air.

Sunday, 3 August

THE NORMALITY

IT'S AN ENDLESS GAME. Nothing but a game. Last night Israel announced the termination of its operations in Gaza. But tonight four people from one family have been killed and others injured while asleep in a house that they fled to in my father's district. Death followed them from Beit Hanoun, where they had lived peacefully for so many years, and tracked them down in Jabalia.* Death wouldn't let them go, knew where to look for them, followed their every footstep. The family had rented this house a few streets away. Last night death decided to put an end to that particular game of cat and mouse. The rocket struck the very center of the house, bringing the whole block down with it. Concrete, shrapnel, bricks, great twists of iron, shards of glass—all collapsed into the same hole—announcing the end of this family.

The electricity comes on at about 1:30 a.m. Everyone in the house jumps from their beds. This is now a regular custom. All the kids start charging their mobile phones. I plug in my laptop. My father-in-law checks the water supply. If it is low he has to turn the water pump on to fill the tank on the roof. Tonight is one of the few occasions when both the water supply and the electricity are working at the same time. My mother-in-law starts washing all the

---

*The Wadhans family lost twelve members over the course of the war. Some were killed in their house in Beit Hanoun, some in Jabalia Camp.

clothes. Everybody tries to make the best of the electricity before it goes off again. We know we have two hours at most. I'm still feeling ill; activity rushes backwards and forwards in front of me like a scene from a movie. I can barely stir from bed. I just want to sleep.

We have grown used to explosions sounding like they're just next door; we no longer jump to the window to figure out who's been hit and then head out into the street to help. Now so many such explosions can be heard. From one hour to the next, you simply wait in the darkness for the dawn to shine a light on the question of which building and which family has been destroyed.

Everything becomes normal. The barbarity of it, the terror, the danger. It all becomes positively ordinary. The only real worry you have, after so many weeks, is a nagging feeling that this war is never going to end. Inside this fact, hundreds of other facts reside. You might die. Your children might die. Your whole extended family might die. You might lose a limb, become disabled. Your house might be destroyed making you and your family homeless. You might lose your friends, your lover. You might be forced to leave your home and live in an UNRWA school or sleep on the street. Individually, however, these fears lose their power over you; they cannot control you. They have taken refuge in the wider, nagging doubt but, outside of that doubt, you become fearless. The sound of explosions becomes the most normal thing in the world; the blinding light given off just before a drone attack—normal. The constant hum of the drones—normal. The sound of an ambulance screeching round a corner or skidding to a halt—normal. The cries of mothers, the shouts of rescue workers—all perfectly normal. The Israeli army's recorded message on your mobile saying that you stay where you are at your own risk—utterly normal. Waking up in the morning and finding out the house next door doesn't exist anymore—entirely normal. Funeral processions passing in the street below almost every hour—thoroughly, implacably normal. Having electricity for one hour a day or not at all for five days straight—normal. Carrying water by hand up three flights of stairs to fill a small tank on the roof. Forgetting what day of the week it is, what date it is . . . all normal, verging on mundane.

We have to form new habits. As time passes, we realize that these are not fleeting exceptions or one-offs. They will be the routines and habits we must live by for a month, two months, six months. At the beginning of the war, in the first days of July, I thought this would only be for a few days more. After the first week passed, I told myself one more week, just one more. Two weeks in, I told my wife, Hanna, "Don't worry, just a few more days, that's all." We keep shifting our guesses and, before we know it, we are talking months, and the war still looks young and lively. It's not going anywhere. We might not have many days left but the war has got plenty of life still in it.

Despite the Israeli army's declaration that the people of Beit Lahia and the Bedouin Village should return to their homes, most of them don't return. It is hard for them to trust any such declaration. The organizer of the UNRWA school shelter across the road said, as he did the day before, that it is up to the people whether they to choose to return home. They can continue to stay in the schools. A few families decide to return. They prefer to be back home. My cousins were among the people who decided to return. Nowhere was safe for them, after five of them were injured when the UNRWA school was struck. My younger brother, Mohammad, who is pursuing his academic studies in history in Cairo, phoned to tell me that Sha'bban, one of our cousins, has arrived at the Palestine Hospital in Cairo. He visited him last night with some Palestinian friends.

Jabalia has become impossibly overcrowded since displaced people from the northern parts of the Strip arrived. When you walk in the street, you see people from everywhere in the north: from Beit Lahia, Beit Hanoun, the Bedouin Village, Ezbet Abed Rabbo, and Etwam. The streets are full of these people. Most of them are staying in the schools. The lucky ones have relatives in Jabalia to stay with. Either way, every house in Jabalia is currently hosting three or four families. Thousands of people wander in the streets, their trauma palpable. Some have been blinded, some are having difficulty breathing, some look lost in a kind of trance, some tremble and shake with every step. All of them offer a picture of catastrophe.

Another funeral passes in the street below. The bodies of three victims are carried on stretchers. You can see from the outline of the flags stretched over them that these aren't bodies, these are body parts—piles of meat gathered after an attack. Slogans are shouted angrily. Then the shouts are swallowed by silence and all you can feel is the pain left behind.

While playing in the living room, the kids have broken one of their grandmother's plant pots. They were running after each other when one of them threw a pillow at the other and hit the pot. This is the worst thing that can happen from their grandmother's point of view. The children fall silent as she moves sadly to fix her plant that's been uprooted. I say, "It is very young. Not to worry. It'll be OK." She does not reply. She is too busy with undoing the wrong.

Sharif, the pharmacist, has become the new family doctor. Hanna took Naeem to see him as he's been running a temperature for a day now. Hospitals don't respond to minor complaints at a time like this. It would be embarrassing to go there with a fever or a headache. People are dying every minute. Sharif is the only option. He guesses each illness and offers the appropriate medicine. The war has made everyone sick, it seems. I feel better today though. I've been taking three kinds of medicine. My throat hurts less and my chest is calmer. I barely cough at all this morning. My friend Mamoun—a former colleague from my days at the Ministry of Foreign Affairs—tells me he has been coughing as well for the last four days. The gas that the Israeli army fired on his place in Khan Younis made everybody in the house cough. This could have a long-term effect. No one knows. When you are dodging missiles for your very life, you don't pay attention to little details like a strange, persistent cough. I want to say, "This is serious; this gas could be threatening our lives as well." But Sharif ignores me. He asks if I have any cold water. I laugh. In this war, the aristocrat is not the person who owns the most amount of land or property; it's the person who has a bottle of cold water. If you had such a bottle, the world would look at you with envy.

The hum of drones has returned; I can hear one hovering over our heads, choosing its next prey. It's very hot. Jaffa is crying. My mother-in-law warns the kids not to touch her blessed plants. I write my weekly article for tomorrow's edition of *Al-Ayyam*. The article starts with the words "We are OK in Gaza." But it's a lie; we are never OK. Nonetheless, hope is what you have even at the worst of times. It is the only thing that can't be stripped from you. The only part of you the drones or the F16s or the tanks or the warships can't reach. So you hug it to yourself. You do not let it go. The moment you give it up you lose the most precious possession endowed by nature and humanity. Hope is your only weapon. It always works. It never betrays you. It never has before. And it will not this time. Hopefully.

A NEW TRUCE

I WAKE UP listening to conversations in the street outside my window. Everyone is talking about it. A truce is being signed, to start tomorrow morning.

"Are you sure?"

"Yes, the news presenter said."

"What about the tanks and drones? It's quieter today, but you still hear them."

"Only one family killed this morning—in al-Shati' Camp—a few minutes ago."*

"Then they're obviously carrying on!"

"Man, it's a truce. Believe me."

"I might, but that drone up there doesn't."

"You know they are meeting in Cairo today to discuss the cease-fire."

"Who?"

"The Palestinian factions are meeting with the Egyptians, then the Egyptians are going to meet with the American and Israeli delegations."

"And I can return to my home in Beit Hanoun?"

---

*The family of Hamoudi al-Bakri.

"They didn't cover that particular point. The negotiations are about to start."

"What about my home?"

"It is not about your home. It's about the cease-fire."

"I don't care, I want to go back to my home."

The two men continue murmuring under my window. They're standing outside the UNRWA school as the sun begins to show itself from behind a low building to the east.

The talks in Cairo are the main topic on the street. Everyone is discussing the dynamics of the talks, giving his or her thoughts on their likely success or failure. The mere fact that there are talks taking place is happy news in itself. At last there are talks! At last, we can expect an agreement.

The two men, smoking heavily, continue their debate.

"You want your home?! I have no home. Mine was destroyed."

"I know, but at least this means the war will end. I'm fed up with this war. I need to relax."

"Any break in the hostilities will be good. You can congratulate yourself for a moment that you've survived!"

"You can bring your family and stay at mine."

"When I went back to Beit Hanoun, I didn't recognize the street I'd lived on for forty-five years. Everything was changed. Most of the houses have been destroyed. I had to guess several times which was my street until eventually I got the right one. I couldn't work out which part of the rubble was my house. It is good to survive, nonetheless. At least none of my kids have been injured or worse. I spent that day running between shells like I was playing a video game. Like I was a character in the game, someone else was playing me. Any one of the shells could have killed me."

He finishes his cigarette, throws the butt on the ground and squashes it under his shoe.

Beit Hanoun is like the remnants of this cigarette; someone has squashed it under his shoe.

It's early afternoon, and everyone is happy that the truce has been agreed. It officially starts at 8 a.m. tomorrow, but the shelling seems to have stopped already. Hanna wants to go to the souq to buy vegetables and a chicken. She wants to make couscous.

Last night, an F16 targeted a house in Jabalia and eight people from the Nejem family perished.† You get used to this kind of information. Death becomes a normal citizen in our neighborhood. You hear about him the way you hear about somebody you've gotten to know, someone who moved in long ago, and is now one of us. He's no longer a stranger who creeps into the camp all of a sudden and then disappears. He's a permanent resident. His presence is more certain here than ours. All last night, the tanks had been sending us their shells. You hear each explosion like you hear the smash of a glass you've just dropped on the floor. You tell yourself, "No worries. It's OK. It's going to be OK." But you're more worried than ever.

I wake up in the morning and, at first, I'm not even sure if I'm alive. What if I'm only alive in the afterlife? Then I see my kids, my wife, my father- and mother-in-law, and I'm still not completely sure. They might all have been killed with me during the night. How do I make sure? I look around, staring, failing to process that this "nightmare" is not simply a nightmare. Sometimes I wish I was just dreaming, that this was not my life. But often my dreams are more real than my waking hours. What if one of those dreams is actually my life?

Last night, I spent three hours visiting my friends in an UNRWA school that they'd escaped to from the rocket fire of tanks in Beit

---

† Bilal Abdel Karim Nejem, Abdel Karim Nejem, Ahmad Abdel Karim Nejem, Raghad Nejem, Suha Nejem, Shaimaa Qassem, and Wael Qassem, plus one name "unknown" (ages all unknown).

Hanoun. As it turns out, this was my school thirty-five years ago. The moment I stepped across the threshold, I was instantly transported back to my very first day. I cried that day. I filled the school with the sound of my crying from the moment my mother and father left me at the school gates. I remember every detail of that day. Now my school is a shelter and the first classroom I ever sat in is the room in which my friend's family now lives. It's their new home. It's the home that allows them to survive. In that classroom my friend's family, plus the families of five of his brothers and sisters, are all living. They share between them the same little space where I first learned the alphabet. The remnants of pupils' writings can still be seen on the blackboard, not yet erased. Could it be that traces of my own first attempts at writing can be seen under all that chalk dust?

In this new home, they have to find a new way of living, their own way. My friend makes us some tea. In the playground in front of the school, we sip tea while the sun sinks in the west behind the flotilla of warships, still sending their fireballs our way.

I meet my friends Salim and Aed at Karawan Café at 3 p.m. Yes, since the beginning of the war this is the first time that Karawan has opened. Few customers seem to have come out today though. Berri, the waiter, is busy serving some of them when we get there. He has not seen them for over a month. There are the usual questions about bereavements, injuries, and damage. The city still seems in shock. Few people walk in the street. Most of the shops are closed. Only Karawan Café and Kazim, an ice cream parlor, seem to be open today. And even fewer people are in the mood for ice cream.

Al-Jala'a Street, which runs from the very north of the city to its center, is empty. This once lively, crowded street is now just gloomy, dark, and sad. At every corner you see destruction and ruin. War was here, you feel, just moments before. The street was named "Jala'a" in the late '50s after Israeli forces withdrew from

Gaza City, having occupied it for a few months in '56. It means "withdraw" or simply "leave," but now stands as just another sign that they haven't.

A drone hovers over our car. I can see it clearly as I go through all my usual thoughts: we're drawing attention to ourselves; the next rocket is going to hit us, etc. It seems Israel will never leave Gaza. It is always here, even if its soldiers are not visible, patrolling the streets as they did not so long ago. The occupation is now truly twenty-first century—the best drone technology in the world is being deployed up there, just to keep us occupied.

This evening, I phone my colleague, Asmaa al-Ghoul, who contributed to *The Book of Gaza*.[1] An Israeli raid killed nine of her family in Rafah a few days ago.‡ Her voice trails off and she pauses, to stop herself crying, before asking me: "Atef, do you have a sense of when this war will end?" She knows I have no answer. But it is hope that enables us to survive. Hope that gives us the ability to fight our disappointments.

When I return to my place in Jabalia, the remains of the man's cigarette from this morning can still be seen. Like Gaza.

---

‡ Asmaa's uncle Ismail Wael al-Ghoul (sixty); his wife, Khadra Khaled al-Ghoul (sixty-two); their daughter Hanadi Ismail al-Ghoul (twenty-eight); daughter Asmaa Ismail al-Ghoul (twenty-two); son Mohammed Ismail al-Ghoul (thirty-two); son Wael Ismail al-Ghoul (thirty-five); and Wael's daughter Malak Wael al-Ghoul (five), son Ismail Mohammed al-Ghoul (eleven), and son Mostafa Wael al-Ghoul (twenty-four days). (Asmaa Al-Ghoul, "Never Ask Me About Peace Again," *Al-Monitor*, 4 August 2014, http://www.al-monitor.com/pulse/originals /2014/08/rafah-gaza-war-hospitals-filled-bodies-palestinians.html.)

Tuesday, 5 August

THE TRACES OF DEATH

WE AWAKEN FROM DEATH. We return from absence and oblivion, jump down from our crosses, still bleeding, trembling. At first our legs cannot hold us up and we fall to the floor. Then we gather our strength and start to walk. The radio whispers to us that this is not a lie, not just a morning sermon or some kind of prophecy. This is true: we are alive; we have come back from death. Our resurrection didn't need a miracle. It just happened.

Walking the streets of Gaza, you see traces of death on every face. You sense death was here; death came close to this person or that. You feel it in their handshakes. You smell it on them. Their faces tell you that they don't know why they survived. Surviving the war is a lottery; these people happened to have won it. Some 1,900 others haven't. The wrong part of the paper was crossed for them.

No one is happy. No one really believes he or she made it. "It wasn't my choice," we say, "because I didn't have any choice at all in this." We were objects that the machine of war just played with. The drone operator must be annoyed that his little video game has been paused for now. Now he looks at us on his screen and kicks his desk, waves a fist at us: "This is not the end of the game!"

Three days of cease-fire have been declared, during which Palestinians and Israelis are going to discuss a permanent peace under the auspices of the Egyptian president in Cairo. This will be the longest truce so far, if it lasts. The feeling is that either both sides will succeed in finalizing the terms of a permanent truce or they will extend the cease-fire to a week, to give them time to reach such an agreement. In which case, we are all finally going to have a break. A real break. During the last month, breaks have been short and scarce and the best of them were called merely "human-itarian" breaks. In war, you learn the importance of small differ-ences. Small semantic variations make a world of difference. One ill-chosen word can destroy a cease-fire and set fire to an entire city. This time, I can say with confidence that we are not having "a humanitarian truce"; there is an actual truce that may or may not become permanent.

I try to explain this to my kids, in particular my second oldest, Mostafa. The main question for him is "Has the war ended?" My answer is unsatisfactory. I say, "It's ended but we're not sure yet if it's ended forever."

"So they might attack again?"

"Not within the next three days."

"Are you sure?"

Of course I'm not sure. But I have to pretend just to calm his nerves. He knows I'm making it up though. He smiles then turns to the window. Some displaced families have started to evacuate the school across the road. In a few days' time, three weeks of dis-placement will be mere memories to them. They don't have much to carry back, just a handful of hopes: that their homes still exist, that there is still a place they can call their own and build a shelter in at least; that the farmland they worked or the jobs they had can be saved. The movement in the street, streaming out of the school, indicates a genuine change in people's hearts and minds; there is a new energy in the air.

For Mostafa, this is better than any of my assurances. Happily, he points to streams of people leaving: "They're going home!"

"Not all of them," I point out. "Some are staying."

The UNRWA man can be heard through his loud-hailer ex-plaining to residents that those people from Beit Lahia, Attarta,

Tel Azaatar, and Jabalia's outskirts can return to their homes. They have to leave the school. People who live in Beit Hanoun can do so as well. The school will now only host those whose houses have been destroyed and cannot be lived in. He promises that a special committee will pay field visits and determine the safety of partially bombed buildings. Many people are not yet convinced; they want to stay. A month of non-stop, merciless bombardment has made them doubtful of the war ever ending. For them, war has become an everyday song, forever playing in the background. Drones, F16s, warships, tanks: these are the instruments of the orchestra, playing the new song of their lives. The UNRWA man has to repeat himself over and over about the need to evacuate the school: "Only those whose houses have been destroyed can stay!"

Today Hanna puts up no argument. For weeks she's been complaining about the kids visiting the Internet cafés next to my father's house where they love to play computer games all day. But this morning, she seems genuinely happy. Today is the first day she's felt safe, she says. And the kids quote her words straight back to her in their case for visiting the Internet café. "Come on! Look at the people in the street!" Talal says. For once, they don't need my help in this argument; they win, hands down.

In Beit Hanoun things are turned upside down. I go with a group of friends to see the state of things. Some things are difficult to believe. All photographs and TV footage of the destruction fall short of what you actually see. All the media reports and firsthand accounts fail to come close to the reality of it. These words now, and any words written before, fall short of the truth. The truth is harder than anything I or a journalist could convey.

By chance, we meet Nafiz, a friend of mine from this village-turned-town-turned-bombsite. He is standing in the ruins, staring at the desolation of his house, almost laughing. A three-storey farmhouse has been flattened, the way a big box of cigarettes might be, squashed between two hands. Nafiz is a crop farmer. His six tractors, two cars, and one large seeding machine that he co-owns

with his two brothers have all been damaged, probably beyond repair. Every other building in the vicinity has also been reduced to
rubble. In the middle of the debris of one building, a hen can be
seen pecking at the rubble, as if convinced of some food underneath. One of her legs has been pinned down by falling rubble. We
manage to release the leg and carry her to some food. She looks like
us all, not quite believing that she made it. This chicken was the
only living animal we saw in our four-hour tour of Beit Hanoun.
We left Nafiz looking at his house in disbelief. Unable to believe
that he has to start his life from scratch.

There is little point writing about the brutality and vulgarity that
has befallen Beit Hanoun. No phrase or metaphor, no rhetoric
can be quite honest enough or do justice to it. If a prophet were
to wander into that town, he might issue a decree: "Your crosses
are still strong, climb back on them so that the birds might eat
your brains."

I haven't felt well all day. I'm covered in sweat, tired and exhausted. I feel old. The war has aged me, turned me into an old
man. I have no appetite, as if my body has yet to be convinced that
normal life has returned. My friend Ibrahim, who was released
from an Israeli prison after twenty-seven years, often describes
the strangeness of his first month of freedom. He says when he
first bought fruit from the souq, he spent half an hour touching
them, telling himself, "This is a real orange; I'm really buying it."
When he slept he kept the door and all the windows wide open. He
needed to make sure that he was not still in a prison. For a long
time, he would have lapses in concentration and forget that the
things happening right in front of him were real.

That's me today. I know exactly what Ibrahim must have felt.
Everything around me insists that it's true. Only my better sense
whispers: "Wait and see."

A MATTRESS
IN THE RUBBLE

TODAY IS THE second day of the truce. Talks continue in Cairo and the thoughts and hopes of every Gazan are there in the negotiating room with them. Every conversation on the street is about what's happening in that room. People exchange updates, expert analysis, their own speculations about what's being said. But everyone's fear is the same: that the conversation will break down and the machine of war will return, to carry on picking us off, one by one. Any update, any tiny morsel of news from Cairo can change everyone's mood. An optimistic statement by a politician or even a journalist can make our day.

Tension and uncertainty prevail, but life—for once—resumes the appearance of normality. The center of Jabalia Camp is full of cars. The moment you start your engine, you're in a traffic jam. Cars come at you from every side. Not only cars but also motorcycles, bikes, donkeys, horses, even three-wheeled bicycles! It looks like a montage of different historical footage—from the same city, but many different time periods. Cars queue up outside the gas station near the corner of the square. Farmers have returned to their farms, fresh produce is finally returning to the camp. Suddenly there's fresh food again. Potatoes, cucumbers, tomatoes, eggplants, zucchinis, green peppers—all of them have appeared in the stalls of the souq, glistening and inviting. Not all the farmers have returned, however; those whose land is situated close to the borders won't risk returning until there is a permanent peace.

My kids ask a question and demand an answer: "When will we return to our home?"

"Soon."

"How soon?"

Hanna, in turn, also wants clarification.

My friend Hisham, whose family is currently staying in our apartment while we stay at my father-in-law's, says that they're planning to head back home soon, to Beit Hanoun. But he doesn't want to risk it until the negotiations have concluded, until he knows for certain that Israeli tanks won't return in the night to flatten them. "No worries," I tell him, over the phone. "It's better to wait for another couple of days." Fortunately, his house was only partially damaged. A shell destroyed most of his living room on the first floor; much of the furniture caught fire, all the windows and most of the doors have been smashed. Relatively speaking though, his house is fine—it's been declared safe. As people say, "Our position is better than many, worse than a few." You have to be happy that you're safe and that you have a place to stay, even if it needs a bit of work. A lot of people don't even have a wall left to shelter under. Their houses are gone.

My friend Nafiz told me today about his uncle, whose house in Beit Hanoun has been completely destroyed. His uncle ordered all his sons to clear the bombsite where his house had stood, and after several hours of work to move away stone and twisted metal, a small space appeared in the middle of the rubble. The uncle then threw a mattress down and just lay down on it. Now he refuses to move. Eventually he asked his sons to bring him a tent and to pitch it around him. Nafiz imagines everyone in Beit Hanoun must be doing the same thing. A town that was flourishing a month ago has been reduced overnight to a camp, a city of tents. Palestinians have the same image of their entire country, as it happens, burned into their memory after the 1948 war: an image of an entire nation of civilized people reduced to a sea of refugee camps, stretching as far as the eye can see.

My grandmother Aisha, a well-educated, prosperous woman of the coastal city of Jaffa, suddenly found herself, at the age of thirty-five, having to live in a tent among the hot sands of Gaza with tens of thousands of other Palestinians. When I look into the eyes of my little daughter, Jaffa, who not surprisingly looks just like my grandmother, I tell her that her fate will not be that of Aisha. She will not be a refugee anywhere. And yet at night, my most common nightmare during this war has been of me, running between shells and explosions, carrying Jaffa in my arms.

Aisha learned from the 1948 war. When the Israeli army occupied Gaza in 1967, her husband—my grandfather Ibrahim—wanted to leave Gaza and take refuge in Jordan. She refused. She told him that she was not going to "drink from the same glass twice." She was not going to flee, or take refuge, anywhere again. She was staying in Palestine. Thanks to this strong woman, I was born in Palestine, not in a refugee camp outside it. Ibrahim took his second wife and all his children—except one, my father, who wanted to stay with his mother—and moved to Jordan, where he died.

When the tanks got close last week and their shells started landing in the narrow streets of my neighborhood, I began to think the nightmare of running through the streets with Jaffa would come true, only I would be running through the streets with all of my family. I wasn't being neurotic; this is what happened to four hundred thousand people last month. It just hasn't happened to us yet.

My friend Nael Shalaiel, from al-Nadi Towers, phones me and asks if I know of an apartment he can rent. He owns two apartments in al-Nadi complex, but both were destroyed. The whole block was brought down. He's currently at his parents' place but he needs an apartment to live in for the foreseeable future, until his apartment block is completely rebuilt. This might take two years, he says. "If we're lucky."

There are thousands of stories like this, wherever you go. The people do not seem to believe what's happened. They're still in shock. You feel that they're moving around without really focusing on anything, that they're only now beginning to recognize the city around them. And yet they still can't celebrate their survival, not yet.

I feel I need to escape from all of this. I want to close my eyes and cover my ears and sleep, and not wake up until it's all finished. I don't want to hear about the woman in the UNRWA school across from my window, going to pay her son one last look. The corpse of the boy was found under the rubble of her home. Part of the family escaped before the house collapsed; others did not. I do not want to see her black tears, sitting on the side of the street across from me. Yes, her tears are dark, made of black water. I can no longer bear to see the worry in Nafiz's eyes when he looks at the future, how he's going to cope with no house, no tractors to tend his field, no car. I do not want to see the pain in the face of the old man and his family down the street, who live now in what used to be his son's shop after their house was erased. I do not want to constantly hear the drone above me, busily trying to calibrate its distance from me. I do not want to listen to the news. In one month, I've heard enough news for a lifetime. I can recognize the voices of the reporters and the areas they are reporting from; I can guess the way they're going to deliver their next statement. I feel like I've heard their voices more than I've heard my own in forty-one years.

I just want to close the window of my room, shut my eyes, put cotton buds in my ears, and lie down, softly, to sleep.

Thursday, 7 August

UNKNOWN SOLDIER SQUARE

I FEEL I NEED TO WAKE UP EARLY. As early as possible, so I can make the most of the truce. Imagine if I slept right through it! Sleep is a precious thing in this war—if you manage to get any at all during the nightly air raids, you still wake up early, surprised by your own survival. On mornings like this though, after a relatively calm night, it's very tempting to sleep for as long as possible. Get it while you can—if the truce isn't extended, it'll be the last proper sleep you get for a while. It is a dilemma. Make the most of the day, or make the most of sleep.

Last night, I went with my friend Ramiz Abu Safia, a promising young diplomat, to one of the cafés in the Italian compound in the Nasser quarter of Gaza City. Ramiz, who is waiting for the Rafah border to open, has been given a post in the Palestinian embassy in Amsterdam. He's never wanted anything quite as much as he wants the talks in Cairo to succeed in their call for an opening of that border. Egypt has kept that door shut on Gaza for the best part of a year now. But for Ramiz, everything is ready. He has a visa for him, his wife, and his kid; he has his plane tickets. This is one of his big dreams in life, to work abroad.

In Karawan Café, everyone was silent, even though the place was full. Normally, the place would be mainly full of older men, playing cards and talking about the good old days. Sometimes they would quarrel over who dealt this card or that. Today no one plays cards. No one talks about the past. They talk about a future they're not certain of. Berri, the waiter, is busy preparing the nargilahs for customers. His face is very gloomy. Like everyone, he seems tired and exhausted. War has run his batteries right down. He sits down next to me to smoke a cigarette. His hair is uncombed, he has coffee stains on his T-shirt. He holds his coal tongs in his left hand. He looks deeply in my eyes and asks, "Is it going to start again?"

My friend Mamoun returned to his flat this morning in Tel al-Hawa, a neighborhood on the south side of Gaza City. Like most flats in his building, all the glass has been blown out of the windows. Sitting in front of us now, he is full of anger. He talks for half an hour nonstop, off-loading, listing his disappointments. He cannot believe the scenes he saw in Khuza'a. He declares it a war crime that needs to be punished. Two days ago, on the first day of the truce, he visited the quiet little village on the east side of Khan Younis where some of his family members were staying. He helped search through the debris for missing bodies. As he talks, I can see he is sweating. Aed and I smoke the nargilah quietly, listening to his anger.

Aed, a very smart left-wing intellectual, no less angry than Mamoun, doesn't say a word. When asked for his thoughts, he says, reluctantly, that it's better not to talk. "Words can't express the anger inside." He is right. They're both right. Berri's worry is right. But nobody can help the situation. I have had enough of this darkness. Sometimes, you need to hear some good news. You need the whole situation to prove you wrong, defy your expectations, provide you with a different reality. You need reality to rise above all your worries and prove them false.

In the Unknown Soldier Gardens, a few hundred people have gathered to listen to a politician urging them to remain steadfast behind the military. This angry man stands in the back of a van proclaiming through a loud-hailer: "We are going to win! Israel is going to be defeated!" The politician is promising that the war will not end without results. It's midday and people are exhausted from standing in the sun. Nearby, I can see the Kazim Ice Cream Parlour beginning to fill up with people wanting something to cool them down. Berri, noticing everyone walking back from the gardens, says, "I want this war to end," then stamps his cigarette out on the ground.

So far, the electricity has been on for six hours. This is the longest spell we've had for over a month. The electricity company says it has managed to fix key power lines and infrastructure damaged by the Israelis. It announces its new schedule: six hours a day, beginning today. When you lose something, you realize its importance. I spend the afternoon sitting beside the fan while the sun burns outside. I could sleep, but I don't. I just want to enjoy the feel of what electricity means: fan, breeze, coolness.

It becomes apparent that the talks are not going to bear fruit. The positions of the two sides are too far apart. The more I listen to the news, the more I feel depressed. Everything I hear on the radio tells me that, at 8 a.m. tomorrow, the war will recommence. By the evening, everyone I know starts to lose hope. They become convinced that war is looming once again. The sound of the drone whirring above us solidifies this fear into fact.

People start acting accordingly. Shops close early. Many of the displaced people who had briefly returned to their homes in Beit Lahia and Beit Hanoun begin returning to the UNRWA schools. They cannot gamble with their lives and stay in these well-targeted areas. No one is happy with the news this evening.

I am at my friend Faraj's place, having something to eat, when suddenly we hear gunfire. We all look at each other, terrified. Faraj's son, Wasim, says it must be because the negotiators have agreed to prolong the truce! The shooting must be someone celebrating by firing his gun in the air. Faraj goes out to see what's going on. No one is happy, it turns out. In fact, there is anger in the streets. Five military personnel have been killed in accidents during the day and are being carried to the graveyard, to their final rest. The gunshot was for their passing.

It's about 11 p.m. now. At 8 a.m. tomorrow, in just nine hours' time, the truce will end and we will all go back to war. We are sure of this. I feel tired as I realize tomorrow will be a different kind of day. I say to Faraj, "At least we've had three good days when we could move freely and relax a little." Tomorrow will be different, of course. When you have to live, you need to teach yourself how to die, and when you have to die, remind yourself how to live. This is how we cope with this situation. Now we need to remind ourselves that life is possible, even when the shells and rockets start crashing down on us again, tomorrow.

It's midnight when I get back to our place. Jaffa is trying to sleep. The moon lights the sky. It comes through the window. She has just learned to pronounce the word "moon."

I ask her: "What is it?"

She replies gently: "Moooooooooon."

From time to time, she points to the moon again saying, "Moooooooooon!" She seems happy with her discovery. The light of it illuminates her whole face in the dark, making her hair glint in places. When she came to bed this evening, she brought her latest, treasured possession: a new pair of shoes that Hanna has bought her. She holds them beside her on the bed. Happy with the shoes and looking admiringly up at her new moon, she falls asleep, without Hanna or me noticing.

Friday, 8 August

A NATIONALIST SONG

IT'S 8 A.M. AND THE truce has just ended. I've barely slept. I've been listening to the news all night, waiting for any glimmer of hope that it might be extended. At 6:30 a.m., I got out of bed and looked through the window. In an hour and a half, I thought, this peace will vanish. I went back to bed; everyone else was fast asleep. Even Jaffa, who's normally the first to wake up, carries on sleeping. From time to time, I look at the clock hanging on the wall. Suddenly, a speeding car sounds its horn in the street outside. Then other cars do the same. Hanna stirs. "Maybe it's another truce and they're celebrating," she says. I know better; the beeping of the horns is a signal to everyone that the truce is ending. It's heralding the return of war, warning everyone to be more careful. 8 a.m., on the dot.

I lie there, waiting for the explosions. It remains quiet. Nothing near us, at least. This is good news. I try to go back to sleep. Jaffa is still deep in a dream and I tell myself I need to do the same. But the rest of Jabalia Camp wakes up as normal. People walk up and down the street beneath my window. A man across the street sits listening to a radio; the volume's turned up so loud, we're all listening to it with him.

The reporter talks about explosions in the Zeitoun quarter of Gaza City. An F16 has targeted several houses in the area.

I'm not really awake; my eyes are half closed, half open. The sound of the reporter's voice ebbs and flows like the tide as I drift in and out of consciousness. Sometimes I have to struggle to listen, to pay attention. Other times I have to make an effort to ignore the noise and sleep. Like everything else around me this last month, I'm not sure which part is a dream, which part reality.

"Israeli missiles have struck the Noor Mosque in Sheikh Radwan, Gaza City. Two teenage boys are reported injured. Heavy shelling is also reported near residential areas in Nuseirat Camp, as well as in Rafah and Beit Lahia. Attacks are being reported from air, land, and sea."

After the bulletin, a nationalist song comes on and fills the street, and all the houses nearby, with its passion. I close my eyes. The rhetoric of the song and all its patriotic expressions echo in my head. I imagine everyone in the street marching in sync to it, their knees rising high off the ground and their feet slamming against the tarmac. Their arms move around in the air in time to the music, the rhythm of the song leading them on.

Hanna is on the phone to her cousin Nisreen, who lives in Nuseirat. It's her birthday today. It's a long chat, as usual.

The Friday prayer is now being called. My father-in-law isn't going to the mosque today. It will be one of the few Fridays he hasn't attended prayers. For three days now, he's been suffering from stomach cramps. He subscribes to a theory that it's Israeli gas; that the Israel Defense Forces have been dropping white phosphorous during the night. Over the weeks, I've heard from scores of people suffering from either a stomachache or a sore throat—like the one I had myself a week ago. My father-in-law tells me he had a sore throat as well and talked to his doctor about it. The doctor said it was possibly an infection but he couldn't say why everyone was getting them at the same time. So my father-in-law will miss today's prayers. He can't walk to the mosque on his own. This will upset him, I know. The Friday sheikh is always very angry and promises the people that heaven will reward them and eternal life waits for them, but the people want to hear about this world, now; that a little more life awaits them here on earth, that they'll survive.

Come the afternoon, more attacks are being reported all over the Strip. The realization that "war is here again" catches us off guard. We're aware that some stupid part of our brains still clings to wishful thinking about the truce, even now.

Suddenly there's a huge explosion. Somewhere close. All of Jabalia seems to shake, from left to right. Everyone is afraid. We think it might be in one of the nearby buildings. I go to the window. Hanna goes to another one on the other side of the apartment, while the kids scatter between us, trying different windows to see if they can spot which house has been hit. My son Naeem shouts and points to smoke rising above a rooftop to the south. A thick plume of smoke seems to be spreading from it, across the whole camp. We close the window and stand back, watching, as it silently passes right by the window, heading down the street. Ambulance sirens fill the camp, just as the white smoke reaches the end of the street; the sound and the smoke competing with each other for air.

Later, we hear that it was the house of the Suliman family, near the Jabalia sports club, that the F16 chose to obliterate. Many have been injured.

Our lives are dictated by the rhythm of war and truce, war and truce; it's like a dance, you have to follow it. War decides for us when we go to bed and when we get out of bed. It teaches us to be fully occupied with every detail of daily life. It makes electricity the most important thing in the world, then it forces you to forget there was ever any such thing as electricity. Your mood is bound by war and then, suddenly, it's defined by truce. If there's a cease-fire, you feel like you're on cloud nine. You want to throw a party. Then you hear about the death of others. And you despair again. You remember that it only takes one more strike, one more break in the truce, one more rocket to drop through the sky, adjust its position, fire its boosters, and find you. You start to imagine your whole existence as a bit like a vacuum, something that contains nothing and then disappears the moment it can.

I see anxiety on all the kids' faces. They don't understand this rhythm of war and truce, war and truce. They can't process the logic of it or understand the reasoning behind the decisions. They thought the war was over. How can something that's over start again? How can everything turn 360 degrees in one hour?

"Of course, we are not going to die!" says Mostafa suddenly. I'm not sure if he's asking me a question, or insisting on a fact that he's completely sure of. Nobody understands. We just look at each other from time to time as the bombs drop, to ask an obvious question: "Did you hear that?"

It seems that the whole camp has decided to live with this war, to adapt to it, to carry on regardless of its brutality. When I finally leave the house tonight, at around 7 p.m., the streets are full of people. The shops are still open. Market traders are selling grapes and figs, displaying their wares on every corner of the souq. I wonder if there is some truce taking place that I'm not aware of. "Perhaps a new deal has been struck in Cairo in the last hour?" I ask a stallholder. He interprets my question as a sign that I know something he doesn't, and starts to smile and get excited. Before I get a chance to clarify what I meant, there's a loud explosion to the east of the camp.

I smile and say, "What's the difference?"

Saturday, 9 August

CROSSING THE ROAD

TODAY IS CALM. No explosions so far. Everything adopts the appearance of normality. If you don't happen to be near one of the UNRWA camps, you might not think there was a war going on at all. The sound of drones persists, but that's normal in Gaza regardless of whether there's a war. Everyone goes about their business just as they would in peacetime. You realize how odd this looks. You don't trust it. There must be a catch, some kind of trick being played. A hidden fact you haven't realized. The day feels like an oasis of calm in an endlessly wide desert of war. A mirage, perhaps.

It's midday and nothing happens. I turn on the radio to see if there's any news I don't know about already—you hear every single explosion at night, but during the day their sounds are masked by other noises so you don't hear every one. Also, the more you get used to something happening, no matter how extreme or life-threatening, the less you notice it. For these reasons, I don't trust the silence or the calm. I don't believe it. Likewise, when you're in the middle of an air raid, you don't believe it either. It's unreal, you need to convince yourself it's a dream, it's going to end.

Hanna tells me there was a discussion on the radio this morning about postponing the opening of schools. School term was meant to start on 24 August, but this is impossible for the UNRWA schools at least because thousands of people are currently living in them. They're now looking at postponing the start of the new school year until October, Hanna explains. Naeem listens to this, quietly. Unusually for a boy his age, he loves school. He complains that he doesn't want to have to wait until October before he can go back. Then he asks suddenly: "Are there people living in my school?" Talal and Mostafa's school is run by UNRWA and based in Jabalia Camp near where we're staying, whilst Naeem and Yasser's school is run by the government and located in Saftawi, near our actual home. He is happy when I explain to him there are no displaced persons living in his particular school.

"Then the new term is not going to be postponed!"

For him it's a simple logic and people should follow it. Sadly, it is not going to be followed. I'm grateful it's not me who made this decision. Hanna explains to Naeem that all schools are going to be delayed, but he just protests more.

"What do you miss about school?" I ask.

Everything, he says. His friends, his teachers, even the subjects.

Yasser listens to all this attentively, and then jumps into the conversation enthusiastically: "I want school! I want school!" He's imitating Naeem, of course.

"Do you miss school, too?" I ask.

He doesn't know what "miss" means so I explain it's when you want something that you used to have sooooooooooooooo much. He says, "Yes, I want school sooooooooooooooo much."

I was right to doubt the calm. It's quiet here, but elsewhere, in Nuseirat Camp, an F16 has been feeding itself. The Nuseirat Mosque is now gone. Three people are reported dead. A man riding a motorcycle who happened to be driving away from the scene was killed in a separate strike. The radio goes into great detail. Other attacks are continuing, far to the south in Rafah, and up north in Beit Hanoun and Beit Lahia. I'm just grateful it's not here.

The heat is too much for me this afternoon; I have to lie down. I like the idea of making the most of this calm, doing nothing for a couple of hours, thinking about nothing. But in this heat, even doing nothing is unpleasant; it's too hot to sleep.

Naeem, Yasser, and Jaffa are running around the apartment, making a racket. The three of them are requisitioning various bits of furniture for their game: mattresses, pillows, blankets, bed sheets. They construct what they call "houses"—everyone builds their own using pillows and mattresses for walls and sheets for roofs. They then sit in theirs and communicate with the others from behind the walls. The "houses" game is an old favorite. I remember playing something similar with my brother and sisters when I was a child some thirty years ago. Back then, the Israeli army would impose an endless series of curfews on the camp. Sometimes we would have to stay in our small, hot apartment for a month. The women would sneak out, now and then, in the night, breaking the curfew and risking being shot by the soldiers, just to bring back food from the neighboring town of Jabalia or Beit Lahia. (During the First Intifada the farmers would show great solidarity with the camps and would bring the produce to certain agreed meeting points outside each one.) For us kids, though, it was an unbreakable prison sentence, so the invention of pastimes and preoccupations for the most cramped of spaces became a necessity. It is this necessity that my children are responding to now. Yasser destroys Jaffa's house and cheers at his own success. Jaffa starts crying and it's clear she's not going to stop. I have to get up and help her rebuild.

My recently homeless friend Nafiz is now living in a school like so many others. As the war progresses and the UNRWA schools become full again, the UN is having to rent additional government schools from the Palestinian National Authority.[1] Nafiz is in one of these, near Sheikh Zayed Square, north of Jabalia Camp. He has become involved in the day-to-day running of the refugees' lives in his school. Along with others, Nafiz has formed committees to govern things: to distribute food, to settle disputes as they arise among the displaced, to organize a rota for the guarding of the entrances (in case of thieves and intruders).

I sit with him in a classroom and we're joined by a few friends. He makes us coffee without sugar. Life in the schools is so fraught and its day-to-day business so all-consuming, that, to its occupants, a visit from an outsider is a rare chance to get a glimpse of what's going on in the rest of the world. I might have news or new information. I'm bombarded with questions: What have I heard? What are people saying? What's my analysis of the situation? I tell them what I can, that I think it will need more time. "But soon," I say, not sure if I actually believe that.

On my way back, I make a phone call, and, as I'm speaking, I'm touched on the arm suddenly by a little boy. I assume he's asking for some money so I explain: "I'm on the phone." The boy, around ten years old, keeps dragging at my arm. I finish the call and he starts to mime someone driving a car, turning the steering wheel. I go with him. He takes my arm and we cross the road, quite slowly. Only then do I understand; he is deaf and dumb and simply wanted help to cross safely.

Sunday, 10 August

THIS IS FAME

TONIGHT THE DRONE knocked at our door. It's 1 a.m. and suddenly there's a colossal explosion, extremely close. Closer than the cupboard. Closer than the clock on the wall. I jump out of bed, and start searching around to see if it was inside the house. Hanna wakes up and points to the window. It's dark outside. The full moon doesn't help. Neighbors are leaving their houses and filling up the street already so I run to the door to shout down the hallway, "Are we hit?" Nothing. I run down into the street to get an answer.

Outside, it's no clearer what's happened. Everyone is shouting, trying to work out which building has been hit. Suddenly, in the middle of the confusion, a young man steps out in front of us, covered from head to foot in white dust. He declares it was his house, looking like a ghost, someone who's fallen straight from heaven.

"Which house?" we all ask. Then we see it. The second house from the end and everyone heads over towards it. The ghost says he was sleeping and the next thing he knew, he'd been thrown out on the street. His arms are bleeding and his face is cut, small patches of red against the white. We look at the house. Luckily, the rocket struck close to the stairs, the strongest part, so it hasn't collapsed. We all help with the rescue, using the lights of our mobile phones to see, since the electricity is out and complete darkness shrouds the city.

In the end, three family members are found injured, including a woman who has lost her leg.

I look up to our apartment and see the silhouettes of Mostafa and Hanna in the window. The ambulances arrive to collect the injured and, a few minutes later, calm seems to return completely as if nothing remotely unusual has just happened. I try to sleep. But the usual spiral of uncertainty prevents me: What if death comes now, this minute? What if this thought is going to be my last? Etc., etc., etc. Things look dark outside. I get up and stand by the window. Only the washing hanging outside a small shop, where a displaced family is living, seems to move in the breeze. In a split second, you can simultaneously cease to exist and become a news item. You swap your existence for TV airtime, radio coverage. A rocket hits your bedroom and you feel nothing; it's just a dream, like the one you were having. Only, in this new dream, your body is in lots of tiny pieces that neighbors will gather up in a plastic bag. A few minutes later and you're born again! The radio presenter announces your family name and your age in a breaking news item, although he explains these are only preliminary reports; they need corroborating. A few minutes later, your name appears again—in full this time—in the news ticker along the bottom of the TV screen. If there's a spelling mistake in your name, be patient with them. Don't get angry. This is fame.

And it is a dream, anyhow. A dream that runs under another dream—life—that runs under another dream—the one you were having as you slept—that runs under another—the memories of the past that bubbled up into the dream you were having, and so on. It is endless. It goes on and on, and when eventually you find yourself awake and realize it's morning, you really do get up! You're alive. This is it, you think. You've been spared.

Seven people were killed today, across various attacks on the Strip. Relatively speaking, this is a small figure; previous days have seen more than a hundred killed. This is a calibration you get used to.

Seven deaths is good. The news also tells me that a further ten bodies have been found under the rubble from previous bombardments, where Israeli tanks have withdrawn. There is a kind of math going on that I take solace from: in the first few days of the war, the daily death toll barely reached 20, then it grew to 50. At its height it reached around 120 a day, and now, each day, it subsides. If you follow the line of the graph, sooner or later, it's going to reach zero. There or thereabouts the war will end. Zero is where things started and where things will end. Excluding the truce days, it's a fairly regular curve. If we're lucky it will stay regular and the war will be over soon.

It's a strange education in the value of life. All you know is that if you escape this war with your life, you will live it to the full afterwards. People you know pass away. Others lose their limbs, are crippled and have their ability to live freely taken away from them. My cousin Yehia lost his eyes in the 2008–2009 war. It was 6 January 2009, and Yehia was fleeing with his brothers from their home north of Beit Lahia, close to the Israeli border. They were heading to their sister's house in Sheikh Radwan when an F16 struck the Fakhoura UNRWA School that they just happened to be passing. My cousin was in exactly the wrong place at exactly the wrong time. More than forty were killed; the explosion took his eyes and badly disfigured his hands and legs.[1]

Suddenly, this tall, energetic young man, in his third year in university, had to adapt to a whole new pattern of life. Only his sense of humor gets him through, I think, covering his sorrow with some sweetness. Life without this ability to start again, afresh, must be unbearable.

My friend Abu Suliman is still living in his wife's hair salon. His flat in al-Nada Towers was destroyed and this is his best option: a tiny hairdresser's salon on the edge of the camp. The whole family moved in: three sons, he, and his wife. It looked perfect when they first moved in, but when I visit him today, he fails to hide his feelings about it. He makes some coffee and confides in me.

You cannot live in a place like this, he says. The hair dryers, the wigs, the extensions, the make-up, the scissors . . . a whole world of women's things. At first it was funny. But now they live, day after day, indefinitely in this surreal otherworld, a world of fashion models and brides on the morning of their wedding day, a world of smiles and unlikely haircuts, mocking them.

I tell him things are still uncertain but there might be a three-day truce, starting tonight. He shakes his head. He wants a permanent solution. He doesn't want a cease-fire or even peace if there's going to be yet another war in two years' time. Last time, in the 2012 war, his whole family was nearly wiped out. For three days, they were trapped in their apartment as the shells struck different parts of the building. They refused to leave and nearly died because of it. This time, they were merely humiliated by having to live in this place. But he's had enough. Like me, he's lived through countless wars and has had enough of the absurdity of it.

AN EVER-CHANGING
GEOGRAPHY

MY SON NAEEM ASKS ME, "When we die, do we wake up in the morning?"

Mostafa steps in: "If we die, we carry on living in a way; we really never die."

Naeem needs more explanation: "But if I die now, tonight, in the morning will I wake up and find you all with me?"

It's some question. What happens after death? All our ideas of death are based on inappropriate concepts, of course: a journey into darkness, as if it's the beginning of a new story. For Naeem, it is brutal and horrifying, but he understands it like any other event in life. Like listening to a story at night, or having a fever. It is an event that ends when you wake up. The images of the children in the hospital beds—blood everywhere, screams, tears, the violent measures doctors and nurses have to take to try to save them—are too much for other kids to see. I do my best to stop my children from seeing these images on the TV, when there is power. But they still see them, either on the TV when they watch it on their own, or on the Internet. Talal and Mostafa have their own Facebook accounts.

In the 2008–2009 war, when Mostafa was five, he asked why the ships were firing on our home, which was close to the beach at the time. "Are we going to die?" he asked, and I replied with a very firm "NO." I remember how unconvinced he looked.

"But many people have died."

"Of course," I said, "but we are not going to die!"

He pointed out to sea and the horizon of warships and up to the lights burning through the sky, the rockets plummeting from F16s and drones, and shouted, "Tell them to stop!"

Who can tell it to stop? Who can put an end to this?

Last night, after the kids went to bed, Hanna and I watched TV. At midnight, the newly agreed three-day truce began, meaning we had a quiet night in front of us. It was also the anniversary of Mahmoud Darwish's death. Most of the Palestinian TV stations were playing clips of him reading his poetry and giving interviews. I spent an hour, with Hanna, listening to Darwish's 1983 recital of his famous poem about Beirut.[1] In the audience, all of Palestine's political elite could be seen, including Yasser Arafat. Darwish speaks about life in Beirut, exactly as it is in Gaza now. He describes perfectly the human capacity to cope with war and loss. In the end, he says, the soul locates a well of strength that makes the journey bearable. Darwish is one of the few writers in our national literature, along with perhaps Ghassan Kanafani,[2] who really capture this idea of home. When I read them I feel at home; I feel as if I am reading about myself.

This morning I have to write a piece for a Palestinian newspaper and I get to thinking about the long-term impact of the decades of war Gaza has lived through. The last hundred years could almost be seen as one long continuous war for Gaza, interrupted only by temporary cease-fires, none of them lasting longer than a handful of years. During the British Mandate in Palestine, from 1917 to 1948, Gaza City, like any other Palestinian city—Jaffa, Haifa, Jerusalem, etc.—was a battleground for the national struggle for liberation. Many famous strikes and uprisings took place—in 1920, 1929,

1936–1939 (the famous Arab revolt), and the 1948 war (called the Nakba, or "catastrophe"). At this point, Gaza suddenly found itself playing host to hundreds of thousands of refugees, descending on this tiny coastal strip from across the whole of Palestine. Suddenly the majority of Gazans were refugees. From that moment on, Gaza was a theater for endless wars: 1956, 1967, the 1970s national resistance, the First Intifada in 1987–1993, the Second Intifada in 2000–2005, the 2008–2009 war (or, as the Israelis called it, "Operation Cast Lead"), 2012 ("Pillar of Defense"), and now this one ("Protective Edge"). War after war after war. The tale of this territory is a tale of wars: a dozen in less than ninety years.

Having written my piece for the newspaper, I head out of the flat to meet my friend Mamoun in Karawan Café. As I walk and think about this long, sorry history, it isn't the number of wars that worries me.

Gaza City's key features change with each war. Every time the war machines roll up to feast on the city once more, they do not scratch at its face or scrape at its skin, they devour whole parts of it. Consequently, Gaza does not have a permanent shape or look to it. What's more, with every conflict, a different, distinctive feature of the city is removed. In the 2008–2009 war, the Saraya Compound was eliminated through scores of F16 attacks. The Saraya Compound was the old military base for the British army in the first half of the twentieth century. After that it became the headquarters for whichever military authorities governed Gaza. It was one of the few places in Gaza the outside world recognized or referred to. Now it's just empty scrubland with a few scraps of grass growing among the sand-covered foundations. What remains of it is the name. People refer to the nearby junction as the Saraya Crossroad. Opposite the Saraya Compound used to stand Gaza's Civic Compound, a place known as "Abu Khadra." In the 2008–2009 war, and again in the 2012 war, this compound, which hosted all the headquarters for all the government's major public services, was reduced to dust. Nothing remains of it. Even the grass hasn't started to grow there.

Add to these, now, the new government compound in Tel al-Hawa, where a tall office block was recently constructed to host the core government ministries—the Foreign Office, the Treasury, the Work and Construction Office, and several others. This compound led to the construction of a whole new quarter of the city. This too has gone. Also, Ansar, which used to be an Israeli prison before being converted to a military base, close to Arafat's house and office—now also gone.

As you walk through the city, you're constantly reminded that this part and that part have changed. You know your children will never know what used to be here or there, or what was here or there before that. The endless wars have prohibited the city from growing in any one direction. Someone who moved away from Gaza ten years ago and then returned would not recognize it, let alone someone from one hundred years ago.

At the Karawan Café, I wait for Mamoun, who's late. He texts, saying he's trying to buy food for his family. There's a truce today so everyone is running around trying to stock up on food and basics for the next stage of the onslaught. I sit with Hussain al-Asmar, a theater director who put on a couple of plays of mine in the past. Hussain looks depressed, worn down by the weeks of uncertainty. He tells me that, during the war, he has been thinking of writing a monologue about a woman who loses her house. He wrote two pages of it but then couldn't continue. He cried and tore the thing up. Another friend, Soud Mohana, also a prominent theater director, joins us. Soud has lost a brother and a niece in this war. They were four meters away from him when they were turned into nothing by a rocket. It was a miracle that he survived. He adjusts his hat, and looks down at the ground, as if trying to see something down there. The three of us smoke nargilah and exchange looks, and silence, while Berri moves around quickly in the background, catering to the demands of a crowded café.

THE TYRANNY
OF WATER

MY FATHER-IN-LAW IS busy this morning, filling every pot in the house with water. He organizes his entire day around the water supply. At the moment there is no power and he is worried that the water tanks on the roof are half empty. When the electricity and water supply fail to coincide, he always predicts an imminent shortage (the tanks need power to be pumped full again). The best way to avert this disaster, he always says, is to store water in as many places and ways as we can—pots, bottles, saucepans. His life is a series of calculations. Sometimes, these calculations don't appear to make much sense when you're not as close to the fine details as we are. Water is just one of these details. Every day, you also have to keep an eye on your gas cylinder. You have to charge your laptops, torches, mobiles, and all electronic devices whenever you have electricity. You have to check if the fridge is still working despite the surges in the current. You have to buy bread for two days as the shop may not be open tomorrow, or the queues too long. You have to keep your drinking water fully stocked and so on and so on.

We all have a long list of such duties that we must perform every day. If we forget any, everyone suffers. In the chaos of war, it's also very likely that you will forget one of them or one of them becomes impossible. You can't have everything. This is one of Gaza's great lessons: certain things cannot always be achieved; demands cannot always be met. We just have to do our best. This is what my father-in-law is doing when he makes all his calculations every morning. He is doing his best. If one of us is derelict in our duties, no one can have a shower for a week. The energy he finds, that all Gazans find, to keep everything going is miraculous. We are surrounded by death, but the only thing Gazans can think about, in their never-ending, daily calculations, is life. Surrounded by death and destruction, we demonstrate the genius we have for living.

Today is the second day of the truce, the second main truce of the war. There's a rhythm to these three-day cease-fires. On the first day, we hardly dare believe it's happening, and spend half the day wondering if it's going to be observed, if it's really any safer. Only by evening do people start to relax. On the second day, we start to adjust properly to the idea that death is taking a break. He's not satisfied yet, but he has to retreat and keep his distance for a while. In the morning, people go out, shop, begin to get a glimpse of their former lives. However, come midday, our thoughts already start to turn towards the next day, tomorrow night, whether it will be extended. The pleasure we expected to taste on these days of peace is spoilt and contaminated by the doubt, the worry, the dread of death's return. The best soothsayer in the world couldn't give you an inkling of what's to come.

It's like watching a horror movie and the lights have come up for a short intermission. Our whole life is this movie and a truce like this is just a chance to stock up on popcorn and drinks. Imagine if the screen freezes on the dimly lit, wide-eyed face of the monster. You get up to go to the bar, buy some snacks, go to the toilet. But the face follows you, its mouth still open, caught mid-scream. You think you hear screams in the sound of water cascading, when you pull the flush. You hear it in the sound of the cash registers. You feel the eyes of the monster as you walk back down the dark corridor into the movie theatre again. You realize that taking a five-minute break in the middle of this movie didn't help at all.

Jabalia Camp is very crowded today. The policemen are struggling to marshal the traffic. I get a taxi to Beit Hanoun with some friends to pay our condolences to my friend Eisa, whose father passed away. No funeral. No gathering. Just a few friends. The city makes me think of those scenes in the Bible and the Koran, of Doomsday. We look over the devastation and, in the middle of it, I spot Nafiz. He has pitched a tent in the middle of the rubble of his destroyed home. When I see him, he is sitting in the porch of the tent with his family, having lunch. From a three-storey house with a garden, to a tent. Nafiz's story sums up the catastrophe that has befallen Gaza. If you look around, you can see people scattered through the rubble, almost as far as the eye can see, picking through the debris, looking for things that might have survived. A boy nearby is looking for his school books, he says. Nafiz asks us in to his tent and he talks to us about the future he now faces. A future without a house or a job; a future that was destroyed when his home, his tractors, and his animals were destroyed.

In the evening, Naeem and Yasser say they want shawarma for dinner. Normally, I'd take the kids to a restaurant for a treat, for shawarma or kebabs, about once a week. They haven't been out of the house for three days, and we haven't been to a restaurant for thirty-six, they tell me! We opt for one of my favorites—al-Souri, meaning "Syrian"—in the center of the camp. The restaurant is packed. Afterwards, I take the two of them for a walk around the streets. Naeem asks happily: "Dad, has the war ended?"

"Insha'allah," I say.*

"It must be. People are out, and we are out!" he concludes.

---

* "God willing."

When we get home, the news reporter tells us warships have shelled the Beach Camp. They have broken the cease-fire.

But Gaza carries on as before. The streets are still full of people. Cars can be heard late into the night. The city goes on filling the apartment with its noise.

Wednesday, 13 August

A PATCH OF WI·FI

ONCE AGAIN, talk about the cease-fire is everywhere. Wherever you go, people are discussing it, giving their predictions, offering theories. The success or failure of it is a matter of luck, of course. There's no art to it. And it's always the same: countless opinions, hours of argument, days of commentary, weeks of analysis, expert after expert, context after context and no result. Today is the third and final day of the talks. By midday today, the truce will end and escalation will be upon us.

Hanna is already addicted to the news but, increasingly, it's the Internet that dominates as her source, rather than radio or TV. She updates me on every development, quotes every statement as if by heart, knows every source. She is the expert on it, but none of it is any good to her, none of it is the news she's looking for.

The children have discovered a wi-fi signal in the house. It belongs to Hanna's cousin who lives in an apartment next to my father-in-law's. However, the signal is only detectable from a corner near the stairs. They have to put a small table on a big table and then a chair on top of that, then stand on the top and reach upwards to catch it. The whole day has been one long celebration of this discovery. They ascend their little chair-table mountain every quarter of an hour and reach up from the summit to make their connection, send and receive. I'm tempted to try it with my own laptop. But I'm scared of dropping it.

Mostafa begs his mother to let him spend the day in my father's place, as usual. The same old argument. Hanna holds her ground but Mostafa knows all her reasons before she gives them and has an answer for each one. In the end, he delivers his knock-out blow: "Imagine you don't let me go now and tomorrow, when the truce ends, I get killed by a rocket. You will cry for the rest of your life knowing that you denied me the one thing I wanted." I don't know whether to be impressed by his arguing skills or a little horrified. He has taken Hanna's logic and just turned it on its head.

Talal has been listening to the reports coming in from the Cairo negotiations. He asks me why Gaza is demanding a seaport. "We can have one without asking the Israelis," he says.

"Of course, we could."

"We swim in the sea. The fishermen can bring fish from the sea. So we can make a port in it too."

He is right, but being right isn't enough. "Right" and "just" are words that don't get the same respect in politics as they do in the dictionary.

People will survive, regardless. Even if there is no extension to the truce tomorrow, they know this situation cannot continue indefinitely. Nothing is predictable in Gaza. A war that we all thought would last a week, at most, is now into its second month. So life has to continue.

In less than two hours, the truce will end, and yet still no sign of a breakthrough.

Thursday, 14 August

A NEW EXODUS

LAST NIGHT, a five-day truce was suddenly agreed. This is, by far, the longest cease-fire agreed since the war's inception. Everyone is happy and celebrating that we finally have some more time to relax. Reading the fine details of the negotiation makes me feel a little sick; so much was proposed, so much was rejected, so little was accepted. What matters now, I guess, is that we can have a proper break. One that gives us a chance to reflect on what has happened, to gather our strength, and plan for tomorrow. When you stop thinking about tomorrow, you become disconnected from the energy of life; you start running on empty. Tomorrow is the energy source that makes life bearable.

For now, we're plugged back in.

Crowds of displaced people start to leave the school opposite us and return to their houses. Five days is enough to return and start making a home again, even if that home is half-destroyed, even if it doesn't have walls, windows, or doors. You still can feel home. Knowing it's only temporary, there's an urgency to their departure; you can see it in their faces, rushing to get as much time back home as they can.

From my window overlooking the school, I can see men carrying mattresses, women fixing boxes with string, and boys and girls helping to carry as many belongings as they can, as whole families set off on foot. This should be a moment to enjoy. A little boy refuses to join his father. He is refusing to leave the school and shouting that the aircraft will kill them if they go home. The father tries to convince him the war has ended. The boy points to the sky and narrows his eyes: "No it's not." The UNRWA officer is giving one of his endless speeches through a loud-hailer, this time explaining that only people whose houses are completely destroyed can stay.

Seeing this, my kids ask: "When are we going back to our place?"

"Soon," I reply, explaining that Hisham and his family are still there at the moment. When they return to their home, we will return to ours.

"We miss our place," Talal says.

I'm not as convinced as the father down in the street that this war has ended. So I explain to the kids that we are staying here, at my father-in-law's, not because the war definitely hasn't ended, but because we want to spend more time with their grandparents. Not a very convincing line, I know.

As it happens, Hisham and his family have decided they are ready to go back to Beit Hanoun. He rings that afternoon to explain he has spent the whole day preparing their house to be lived in again. Some walls have caved in. Several rooms are without windows or doors. "And don't talk to me about the garden," he says, which is now completely treeless. The peach trees, olive trees and apple trees have all been flattened by the tanks. Even the jasmine tree that hugged the exterior of the house is choked with dust and snapped. Eight hours of work clearing the rubble and the house is just about ready to host them again. Hisham explains, over the phone, that they're ready to move in. I tell him this might not be the right decision; he should wait and see what happens in Cairo. But he insists the sooner he moves back, the sooner he can start fixing things properly.

"You can do this when it's over," I say in vain. "But not now."

In the evening, he comes by my father-in-law's place with his wife, to drop off the keys. He looks tired, and appears to be soaking wet. He's just been refilling the water tank, he explains, by hand. He has also covered the windows with polythene, and the doors with bits of material. He has to get started, he says. Unsure if this is the correct decision, I shake his hand to wish him the best, and watch as he and his wife walk out the door and disappear into the street.

Al-Jala'a Street is busier than ever tonight. A man is throwing damaged furniture out of a window onto the pavement outside. On the top of the pile he's created, there's a huge mattress. It lies there as a token, a reminder both of romantic moments shared, and of those that will now no longer take place.

Central Gaza

BACK HOME

LAST NIGHT WAS our first night back at the apartment. It was good to be home. The drones welcomed us, unsurprisingly, with their constant whirring all night long. If you allow yourself to listen to them, you'll never sleep. So I did my best to ignore them, which was hard. In the dark, you can almost believe they're in your bedroom with you, behind the curtains, above the wardrobe. You imagine that, if you wave your hand above your face, you might catch it in your hand or even swat it as you would a mosquito.

Nonetheless, it's still good to be home in our own space. There's something about the smell of it, the texture of daily life as it used to be, our familiarity with the space, the ease with which we relax there, the privacy. Being home makes us realize life goes on.

Hanna has spent the day cleaning the apartment. Hisham's family left the place perfectly tidy but Hanna is obsessed with her belongings and having the apartment the way she likes it. She has decided to go through everything and give it another clean, from the carpet to the airing cupboard. Soap and water are being carried to every room in the apartment. She washes the kitchen utensils, the clothes, the tables, the surfaces. All the bed linen is taken out and piled up. During their stay, only my library was out of bounds for Hisham's family. Hisham kept it locked most of the time but confesses to occasionally creeping in to read the odd book. I missed it myself. I survey the room, so glad to be back in it—the shelves, the desk, the souvenirs, the paintings on the wall, even the imprint of me on the chair from the last time I sat there reading. Being back at home is so calming. It gives me a sense of belonging to something. It feels like we've been away, at my father-in-law's place, for years. It's strange. I used to travel for months on end, but I never felt like this. In the past, I guess, I always knew I was coming back.

This time, I hadn't been sure if the apartment, or worse, if I, would survive. When my grandmother Aisha was forced to leave her beautiful home on the beachfront in Jaffa, she thought it would be only for a few days until the riots and fighting calmed down. She even left the windows slightly open so that the curtains could dance, like a drunken woman, in the breeze coming in off the sea. She didn't want the house to get too hot while she was away. This was 1948. For forty-five years, Aisha waited to go back to that house, to close the windows and relax in the shade of those dancing curtains. She died in Jabalia Refugee Camp without ever seeing them, of course. I have been thinking about Aisha's story all summer, about what it means to never return. After all, nothing is certain in this so-called "holy land."

Today I go to the souq and take Talal and Jaffa with me. Jaffa loves to see the birds in cages there and is always trying to play with them. Today is Friday so I know the poultry corner of the souq will be full: chickens, turkeys, ducks, geese, pigeons, even quails. Not to mention the rabbits. Jaffa will spend every moment she can in front of these wooden cages, poking her fingers inside, saying "Cuckoo . . . cuckoo." She loves them. Later tonight, when she's missing the birds, she'll say "cuckoo" again and again to herself. Today is a real treat for her. She sees hundreds and hundreds of birds. Apparently the farmers are trying to sell all the birds they have left because they know they'll lose them when things escalate again.

Saturday, 16 August

A GAME OF CARDS

I INVITE MY FRIENDS Faraj, Mohammad, Rayed, Ali, and Haytham to play cards at my place. The six of us play *remi*¹ every week, sometimes late into the night. Usually it's a Thursday thing, either at my place or Rayed's. We play and smoke nargilah and talk. It's one of my Gazan rituals. Everyone brings his own torch so, between us, we can light the place up when the power's off. Normally, in summertime, we would relocate the game to the beach, take food and drink with us, and rent a tent late into the night. For the last few years, Israeli warships have fired on Gazan fishing boats every summer, out there on the horizon. We became used to it; they only fired at night, so we would dutifully pack up around 10 or 11 p.m. before they started, lest one of the rockets travelled inland.

Tonight we spend the whole game catching up. Everyone has come laden with stories. I haven't seen Rayed or Ali since the start of the war. Haytham works at the Gazan Municipality and used to live on the same street as me. Ali and Rayed are both athletes and used to play in the national volleyball team. Ali was in an Israeli jail for six years and has only recently been released. He lives in Beit Lahia but has abandoned his house there to share a room with his brother-in-law in the center of town. Rayed lives in Tal Azaatar, which is on the far eastern fringe of Jabalia Camp. He hasn't dared leave his house properly for over a month. It was too much of a risk where he was.

In the morning, I wake with a strange craving for fish. I haven't eaten fish for over forty days. So, with Hanna's permission, I set off for the fish market. I find the place empty. There is no fish in the fish market, it seems. But why would there be? Fishermen haven't dared set sail while the sea is still thick with warships; they haven't braved the waters just as farmers haven't dared to return to their fields with each cease-fire. Although Gaza is a coastal city, it hasn't been allowed to enjoy this fact for almost fifty years. Since the occupation began in 1967, ships from the outside world haven't been allowed to drop anchor at Gaza. Despite hosting the remains of one of the oldest ports in the world—a Phoenician harbor, the ruins of which can be seen on the beach near Balakhia—the city doesn't have a port. Three thousand years ago it had one, but not now. I wrote in one of my stories that the sea is like a nice painting hanging on the wall. It's no more than a painting. You can stand on the beach and enjoy the brushwork, the use of color. But you can't jump into it. You can't take a boat out into it and discover the world. You can dip your feet in its shallow parts; in peacetime you're permitted to go a couple of kilometers out, max, and always under the gaze of the warships. If you can swim, it's only because the warships allow you to, not because it's your right to, not because it's your sea.

Gaza's fishermen face all kinds of challenges in the best of times. When they set out, they have warships, patrol boats, submarines, coastal gun turrets, and drones, all threatening to wipe them out. Not to mention the sea itself. Since 2007, even during peacetime, they have not been permitted to sail more than six kilometers from the shore. Their movement within this tiny slither of sea is a dance with death. During this seven-year blockade, Gaza fishermen have been forced to trade with Egyptian fishermen. Often Palestinian fishermen have to buy what Egyptian ships have caught in waters forbidden to them, then bring their purchase to Gaza. This trade-off takes place out at sea. Only when they manage to conduct this weird, watery exchange do they come home with catches that actually make Gaza feel like a coastal city.

So I didn't eat fish today. It's late now, and, as I write this, I look out of my living room window, westwards, towards the sea. It's almost entirely dark. The only glints reaching me from that black horizon are the lights of warships. Four or five miles out. Waiting for their next meal.

A STRANGE BREED

TRUCE. ESCALATION.

Escalation. Truce.

Truce. Escalation.

Escalation then truce.

Nothing but escalation.

Nothing but truce.

Today is the fourth day of the cease-fire and everyone is waking up to the fact that things may start to deteriorate again, very quickly. Another escalation may be upon us. Over the last three days, people have managed to almost forget the impending return of the F16s, drones, tanks, and warships. They've almost forgotten the fact that this is an exceptional calm, an abnormal peace. But now, even if they're trying to forget it, the news is beginning to remind them. TV stations, radio broadcasts, and online magazines all seem to be talking about the possibility of there not being a long-term agreement tomorrow night. All of a sudden people are angry about losing a peace that we don't even have.

I am at the Hona al-Quds TV studio, being interviewed about life in Gaza during the war and the possibility of a permanent resolution. In Gaza there is one terrestrial TV channel and four satellite channels. I overhear the floor manager explain, off camera, that the electricity generator is about to run out of petrol. The presenter deals with this very cleverly; she apologizes to the viewers that we need to go to an advert break and that we'll be back soon. For twenty minutes, we sit in darkness. A cameraman finds a torch and points it at us while we sit there, casting two great shadows on the wall behind us.

The studios are located on the tenth floor of al-Shorouk Tower, which has been bombarded regularly throughout the war but not enough, so far, to bring it down. The people working in this building are so used to it being bombed they've become quite slow at responding. The building is full of journalists, of course, and they seem quicker to react to danger elsewhere than in their own building. Whenever there's breaking news, somewhere else in Gaza, you see them frantically piling down the steps at the front of that building, desperate for a piece of the action. It's one of those bizarre sights you get accustomed to in this part of town.

Journalists are a strange breed. A friend of mine is a photographer and cameraman. We were once shooting a piece on the roof of the al-Shawa Hosary building, using the Gaza skyline as a backdrop, when suddenly a rocket struck a building behind us. He spun his camera around. The building was quiet at first; it must have been a small rocket. Then a much bigger one plummeted into the base of it, shrouding the entire building in a thick cloud of smoke. "Wow! Exclusive!" he screamed. Like many journalists, he thinks only of work, even at a moment when lives are being lost. His career is built on the suffering of others. This is why many people in Gaza hate journalists and the media in general. They realize, of course, the importance of their coverage, but they know also that they stoke the fire of conflict.

A few days ago, in Beit Hanoun, I saw an old man sitting amid the ruins of his house, suddenly start to shout at a guy filming him: "Stop that! Don't film me! I don't give you permission!" The young man tried to explain that the footage would only do good; it would show the international community the crimes that had been committed and bring more attention to Gaza's plight. The old man, half-angry, half-crying, shouted: "Will this coverage bring my three boys back, or my daughter?" There was no answer. I saw all of this by chance, on my way to see Nafiz. Like the journalist, I have no answer either.

The warships fired on the beach again today. One man was injured. Other incidents have been reported in Rafah and on the beach near Beit Lahia. War is on its way back again. We can smell it. A man on the street tells me the warships are preparing their mortars, in advance, for the end of the truce.

All day, I've been playing with a small piece of paper that I've kept in my pocket for amusement. On one side I've written the word "truce," on the other "escalation." From time to time I take it out and see which side is facing me. It's as good a way of working it out as any. A game of luck, that's all life is anyway. Gaza may be just a juicy exclusive in the eyes of the hungry media. It may be an exercise in town planning that needs to go back to the drawing board, in the eyes of the drone operator. But to me it's a game of luck, improvised on a little piece of paper, thanks to this war.

A DAY ON THE BEACH

IT'S BEEN SIX WEEKS since I've gone to the beach. I share this realization with Hanna, along with the thought that the summer is going to end without me having swum in the sea once. The previous three times I visited the beach, before the war started, I didn't get close to swimming. The first of these was with the family, and I spent the whole time keeping an eye on Jaffa as she paddled at the water's edge. She'd never touched the sea before. It was like a miracle to her. The next two times, I was with friends, talking and watching the World Cup in the beachside cafeteria; again I missed the opportunity.

Usually, we go to the beach every two weeks. We take a big hamper and spend the whole day there, from afternoon to midnight. During Ramadan, this is particularly special, as we break our fast on the beach and then we swim in the sea for the first few hours of darkness. Before leaving, I always visit the fishermen on the harbor wall, boxing up and selling fish, many of which are still alive. I always buy some for the following day's lunch. This Ramadan we missed all this.

Little Mostafa says that if the war doesn't end before the new school term, he will have a swim-free summer too. With this, all the kids start shouting that they want to go to the sea as well. Hanna is not happy with this. She holds up her hand, pronouncing a long, unassailable "NO!" Personally, I think that if the truce ends tonight, today may be our last chance to go all year. Finally, we come to a compromise. Hanna allows me to take Mostafa, Yasser, and Naeem. Talal will stay with his mother. As for Jaffa, there's no way. Forget about it.

I phone Abu Aseel, Wafi, and Faraj, proposing that we all go together. Today there's peace and tomorrow there might not be. They all take to the idea. In two hours, Wafi is transporting us all on his three-wheel motorbike to the seafront. Few people are swimming, understandably. I prepare a nargilah pipe while Abu Aseel takes the three kids for a jump in the sea. Wafi, Faraj, and I sit talking, watching them and enjoying the view. It isn't until the sun starts to set that I realize I still haven't swum yet. I strip down to my trunks and start towards the water, just as it's beginning to get dark. The moment my feet touch the water, two beams of light from the warships swing round and seem to focus on one spot: me. For a moment, I'm completely blinded. Abu Aseel shouts that it might not be worth it, tells me to turn around, walk back slowly. No sudden movements.

Earlier this morning, in Beit Hanoun, I found a piece of paper fluttering about in the rubble. I picked it up. What was written on it was some kind of love letter:

"My beloved, let me wake from my dreams to be greeted by a smile on your lips. Then my day will start with 'I love you' and I will clothe all my feelings with the craziness of your love."

Underneath it were written the names of six girls with phone numbers for each: Faten, Ashjan, Dana, Rana, Nariman, and Manar.

This young boy—the erratic handwriting looked like a boy's—seems to have written his romantic message to all of them! The same message to all six girls. God knows what happened to this young lover, or any of his six beloved girls. I hardly dare to think. I consider ringing the numbers, to see if they're safe, maybe even to deliver his message. I almost do and, for a moment, imagine what I would say to the first name on the list, Faten. Then I abandon the idea. Some stories are best left unexplored. I do not want to hear that he or any of the girls has passed away. It is better to think of him still alive: a young lover, sitting on his bed, writing romantic messages to an outrageous number of girls while Israel assembles the full might of its colossal war machine to target his little home. It is better to think of his endeavor to ignite feelings in one of those tiny hearts, to be deserving of one of them, through a mischievous expression of fake love. Then I imagine the happiness these messages might have ignited in those girls, during such hard times.

On the flip side of the paper, is printed the name of a horror movie, or perhaps a computer game:

The King of Fighters EX2: Howling Blood

Times of terror, times of love. I take this little souvenir of war and archive it in my library, another piece of evidence in the case for life.

In the evening, Hanna discovers that the whir of the drones can actually be of use to her. She suffers from Ménière's disease, an ear problem that gives her a continuous feeling of vertigo and low-pitched tinnitus. The sound of drones is an octave or so higher than the hum of her tinnitus and, now that the drones are almost permanent, the sound of them takes her mind off the Ménière's disease. She laughs at the thought of it: "Thank you, drones!"

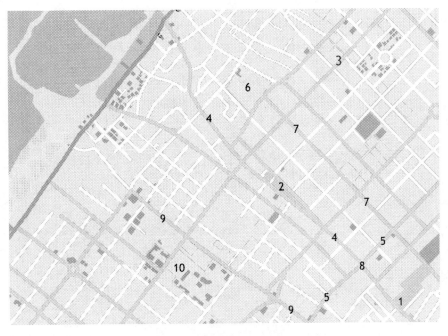

Gaza City

1. The Unknown Soldiers' Square
2. Gaza Municipal Park
3. al-Nasser Street
4. Omar al-Mukhtar Street
5. al-Jala'a Street
6. al-Shifa Hospital
7. al-Wahda Street
8. Saraya Crossroads
9. Jamal Abed El Nasser Street
10. Islamic University of Gaza

THE TUNNEL

ANOTHER STAY OF EXECUTION. Another day of living under the mercy of the extended truce. It's an uncertain life: you're denied any sense of long-term stability but, to compensate, the unseen negotiations give you an extra day. Living without a permanent cease-fire, and knowing one isn't coming, is a bit like walking through a tunnel whose length you don't know. There is barely a glimmer of light at the end; when you think you see something, it's just a glint, reflecting the light behind you. You tell yourself you've been walking so long, it's probably nighttime outside so you might not be able to see the end before it comes. But you don't believe it.

When I sit in the darkness at night, as I do now on my blue sofa, even tomorrow seems a long way off. I mean tomorrow literally. It may be only a few hours away but you can't assume it, you can't plan for it. Instead, if you're lucky, you suddenly find yourself on the other side of the night—in tomorrow—and you realize you've survived another one, but you can't assume you'll survive the next. Tomorrow is still the thing you can't depend on. Instead, you make do with the unending, unbroken tunnel of today.

If you allow your thoughts to wander into events that might take place tomorrow, your predictions are always accompanied by a sense of anticipated disappointment. You know things won't transpire exactly as you predict. Later, if you think back to these predictions, they color both the hopeful past and the unsatisfactory

present. Disappointment has layers to it. And each one has a different taste. The future isn't unthinkable—you just have to anticipate
these layers that will accumulate simply by thinking about it—this
is what we mean by "tomorrow" in Gaza.

My day is like the day of any other Gazan. I wake up in the
morning expecting nothing, planning for nothing; I have no way
of pushing the hands of the clock forward a single second. But
eventually, and without any intervention from me, the day simply
finishes, and, if I'm lucky, the next one comes along with no dis-
cernible difference. We count the days as a measure of how many
days we've survived this war so far but they don't really feel like
different days. Our only consolation is that, as the number grows
bigger, our hope grows that we can survive the rest of it.

You have no power to make the days different. You surrender
to their sameness. Sitting in my living room as my family sleeps
around me, I realize there are only two ways in which the morning
will be any different than the morning before: firstly, if I wake up to
the news that war has ended, news that I have survived, that I can
finally begin to live again! Or secondly, if I don't wake up at all, and
only my friends and loved ones wake up, realizing that the tunnel
just got that much darker.

I have lived with this sense of "untomorrow" since I was in pri-
mary school. I used to love school; it is easy to say this now and to
be proud of it. I used to sit on the floor each night doing my home-
work diligently with my mother helping me. I would look forward
to the simple pleasure of raising my hand when my teacher asked
a question I knew the answer to, and to my answer being rewarded
with his clapping. Tomorrow was something I always awaited with
great pleasure. Then, during the night or sometime around dawn,
an Israeli soldier passing down the street in an armored car would
announce through a loudspeaker: "By order of the military leader
of this district, curfew is imposed. No one is to leave their buildings. Whoever breaks this order puts him or herself in danger."
Thus all my plans for tomorrow were undone. The applause of my

teacher was forestalled. Only the touch of my mother's hand on my head stopped me crying and made me sleep again. But "tomorrow" was abandoned.

So the truce has been extended for another day. Both the war and the permanent cease-fire have been postponed, in equal measure, rescheduled for the "untomorrow."

I head out with Aed to the souq in al-Shati' Camp. Hanna tells me we need tomatoes and potatoes. But when we get there, I suggest that we buy everything in case tonight sees no further progress. Everyone is thinking the same way, buying everything: every type of fruit and vegetable they can get their hands on. Only the meat gets left as there's no certainty people's fridges will be working.

My father-in-law comes to visit us. He brings rice and flour to add to our stockpile. He asks if he can take one of the kids to stay with him—spreading the family, preparing for the worst. The choice is between Naeem and Yasser. Eventually he decides to take Naeem. Yasser cries. In the boys' heads, of course, staying at my father-in-law's means fun: playing with friends in the playground of the school near his house, seeing cousins, and, most of all, being spoiled by their grandparents. Yasser cries for some time after Naeem has gone.

Hanna is busy breaking in the new washing machine that her father, Mostafa, and I bought yesterday. As we drag the old one out of the flat, her father mutters a few words about making the right choice, choosing the right model. We're in luck this morning as the electricity is on and will be on for another five hours. It should give us enough time to do the housework.

In the evening, I go to see Abu Annas, Tarik, and Sohail—my three close friends from Jabalia Camp. We meet at Abu Annas's place. The three of them insist that this time it will be a permanent truce. I say that I seriously doubt it, but they smile, as if they know something I don't. I ask them if they're privy to secret information, but they deny it. Abu Annas says it's just a hunch. I reply that, if it's just hunches and guesswork, we may as well toss a coin to see what our luck holds. Sohail gives me a coin. I tell them heads it is for a permanent truce, tails for escalation.

If it's tails, then they're wrong. More war.

My life, the lives of Abu Annas, Sohail, Tarik, and countless others, has no order to it. Only chaos governs us, blind luck. We have lived so far because of the way the coin has landed each time. As the coin somersaults through the air and then spins on the table in front of us, we sit staring at it, helpless.

Wednesday, 20 August

THE WORST OF DAYS

TODAY IS MY BIRTHDAY. At about 11 a.m., forty-one years ago, I was born in the Jabalia Camp UNRWA clinic. I was the second of ten children. But today, except for the birthday wishes of Hanna, my kids, and a few relatives and friends, there is no sign of a birthday taking place. Usually, I spend this day with the family on the beach. Hanna would make a cake that would be waiting for us when we return from the sea. But, whatever the current circumstances, I feel today is, and should be, a happy day—one to celebrate, even if the situation sanctions against it. Happiness is not something that you find or is given to you; it is something you make.

I ask Hanna what we should do, despite the situation. A few ideas start to be thrown around when Hanna's mobile suddenly rings. It is her dad telling her that the son of my stepmother, Mostafa, was killed in a drone attack this afternoon with his father. Mostafa, my stepbrother, had been on his way with his father to their farm where they were going to tend to a few cows and a couple of Arab horses for the first time since the start of the war. They were on their way to feed animals. They were driving west towards Beit Lahia where the farm is based. It was midday. The rocket hit the body of this thirty-one-year-old man as he was driving a car that carried a pot of water for the horses to drink. His father was seen a few minutes later, lying under a tree at the side of the road;

he was trying to get up so that he could help his son. But then another rocket struck the ground in front of him. My stepbrother was torn to pieces. His body was brought home in a plastic bag. His father lost a leg and an arm, then died on the way to the hospital. Mostafa left three kids behind, as well as a farm full of frightened, thirsty animals.

Hanna goes to the women's funeral to pay her condolences to my stepmother. It is a hot evening. The truce never lasted. Before the sun sets, the aircrafts start their sporadic raids again, in different places across the Strip. The worst is shortly after 10:30 p.m. in the Sheikh Radwan neighborhood of Gaza City, where a house belonging to the Dalou family is destroyed, leaving three dead and forty-five injured.* At the time of the attack, I was being interviewed at the Palestine TV station—as an occasional commentator, I'm sometimes asked for my reading of things. The reporter on the ground was stuttering as he described live what he was seeing. The other reporter from al-Shifa Hospital was sending live photos of the injuries. One of them was a girl a few months old. The image of this girl being carried by a paramedic with a piece of rocket shrapnel still embedded in her little soft skull sums up what we all feel about the brutality of this war.

At around 1 a.m. the previous morning, an F16 destroyed the four-storey house of my friend Tarik. This beautiful, welcoming home, situated at the eastern entrance to the camp in an area called al-Shuhada, is now just a pile of stones. This evening, I walk from my place in the Saftawi area towards the camp. I pass al-Shuhada to say hello to Tarik. He is sitting on a wooden bench in front of the ruins, surrounded by other friends. Words can't convey the sorrow I saw in his red, hot face. As we say in Arabic: if you put an egg on his cheek it would fry. After a warning rocket sent by a drone, Tarik

---

*Wafaa Hussein al-Dalou (forty-eight), Mostafa Rabah al-Dalou (fourteen), and Ahmad Rabah al-Dalou (age unknown). A further two succumbed to their injuries.

and his family had fled, and three F16 rockets struck ten minutes later. As we talk, Tarik frequently turns and looks back at the rubble of the house he inherited from his father, the house that had witnessed his childhood, his youth. He needs to remind himself that it's true. He had built on this house, expanded it, making it four storeys high, so that he could share it with his brother and his two married sons. Now it's all gone. Relegated to the past, like the pages of a story.

The homing pigeons that Tarik keeps on his roof have also lost their home. Around twenty of them circle above us, trying to figure out where their roost has gone. They do not understand the language of human destruction or the brutality of war. As close relatives of the dove, they only understand peace. After a while they land, perching on boulders and bits of wall. They seem lost, not knowing where to go or where to sleep. Tarik has moved with his family to his father-in-law's house; these pigeons have no fathers-in-law to go to. Sitting there we suddenly feel the fate of lost pigeons, homing pigeons without a home. What do they whisper to each other now as the sun sets, like a great orange over the sea?

When darkness eventually throws its cloak over us, Tarik's friends start to leave. I have to go too. I suggest he leave as well and go to his father-in-law's. The thought occurs to me, in all seriousness, that he might die of sorrow. Every look he casts over the rubble kills him. He refuses to leave. He tells me he needs to find a way to feed his pigeons.

I go to my stepbrother's house to pay my condolences. Everyone is silent. Tears have not yet dried on the cheeks of his children. Afterwards, I go to my father's place to see my stepmother. She is still at the women's funeral. When she arrives at around 9:30 p.m., she looks exhausted. Sadness is painted all over her face. She can hardly move. She lies in bed with tears still silently running down her cheeks. My dad brings her grapefruit juice, which she does not drink. Silence reigns.

My dad suggests that I go home soon as it is dangerous to walk in the street too late, or else sleep at their place. I prefer to go home. As I walk through the camp I'm accompanied by the drones' usual whir. It's now forty-five days since the war started and everyone has learned the rhythm of war. People are acclimatized to it, know how to read its detail. More people walk in the streets at night; more cars are passing.

I arrive to find everyone already fast asleep in the corridor. There's no electricity now, so I sit with a small candle in front of my laptop as I write these last few words of today's entry. Today was my birthday.

Thursday, 21 August

THE HISSING OF SNAKES

THIS AFTERNOON I take Jaffa to the hospital. Over the last week, she has been complaining about her eyes hurting her. They look red and the irritation means she won't stop scratching them, making them worse. Sharif, the pharmacist, gave me an ointment that Hanna had been advised to use by a doctor at the UNRWA clinic three days ago. But the ointment didn't seem to help. Jaffa's eyes didn't improve. I have decided to take her to see a specialist at the al-Nasser Eye Hospital. It's only ten minutes by car from my place, but Jaffa is still excited at the prospect of going out. When I tell her, she rushes to the small cupboard near the door, where we keep the shoes, and brings back my shoes.

In the whole hospital, there are just two doctors. Everyone else has been posted to the other larger hospitals to care for the injured; many of them have head wounds and need urgent operations, including eye surgery. The two remaining doctors have to look after an enormous number of patients. After waiting half an hour, I enter the doctor's office. He plays with Jaffa for a few seconds while trying to figure out the cause of the illness, then he writes a prescription that I have to take to the hospital pharmacy. I find the pharmacist outside, sat in a chair under a large tree, painting her nails. I give her the prescription but of the three medicines written on it, she tells me, there is only one in stock.

Hospitals suffer at the best of times in Gaza, from a short-age of equipment, medicines, and material needed for surgery. At times like this, doctors have to work under extreme pressure; often the same team of surgeons will conduct five surgeries on five different patients at the same time. Gaza's hospitals are not staffed or equipped to receive the kinds of numbers they've seen over the last month and a half. Add to this restrictions on movement for staff and the difficulties of transporting materials, medicine, or patients during the Israeli bombardment, and you realize things couldn't really be much worse. I thank my stars I didn't have to take Jaffa to one of the general hospitals and she was spared from seeing those horrors. I buy the other two medicines from a pharmacy nearby.

Whilst I have been with Jaffa, Hanna has been at the women's funeral as it continues into its second day at my stepbrother's place. My stepmother has spent the day there receiving further condolences from relatives, neighbors, and friends.

In the evening, I go to my father's place. My stepmother has just returned from the funeral. Like yesterday, she collapses onto her bed as soon she arrives. No words of mine can lessen her pain. No expressions can extinguish the fire inside her. No sentence I might write here can capture the precise feeling of that moment.

Later, I go to Hussain's place, to smoke nargilah and drink coffee. The camp is quiet except for the sound of the drone. Last night had been a heavy one for Rafah. Seven people were killed in one attack, including the father of a friend of mine, Essam Younis, and his stepmother and niece. Essam is one of Gaza's veteran human rights activists.[1] He runs the Mizan Center for Human Rights. Now he has to defend, too late, the rights of his late father and step-mother. Hussain is very pessimistic. He says the war will take at least another month. The thought of it chills me. He doesn't see why not. We hadn't expected the war to last forty-six days but it has. Why shouldn't it last another month or more?

On my way home, I hear the sound of shells fired by warships, whizzing through the sky. It sounds like the hissing of snakes. The fragrance of sycamore trees fills the neighborhood and reminds me that I'm nearly home.

In the flat, Hanna and my son Mostafa are awake. We chat for an hour before they eventually fall asleep. Everybody is bored of this horror as well as being exhausted, terrified, numbed, sick. We're bored of it. We want to go to sleep and wake up with this nightmare over.

A QUARREL
WITH A GIRLFRIEND

YOU NEED A little luck to get you through war. All wars are unpredictable. You have to learn to live with that unpredictability, subject yourself to its mechanisms, get a feel for it. But on top of this you also need luck. The dead are not military personnel, the traditional targets in a battle. Most of them are your fellow citizens. Some of them are relatives or friends with whom you shared a good portion of your life. You have not made it this far because you are smarter than them or because you took the right precautions. Many of them took the right precautions as well; many of them were smarter than you. But they still weren't a match for the unpredictability of war.

The Balata family decided to relocate from their place on the outskirts of the Strip, to live with relatives closer to the center, thinking that their place was safer. Luck laughed on them as the tanks picked out this new home instead, reducing it to a series of piles—of stone and of flesh. Their flesh. While the house they had fled remained untouched.* The same fortune befell those people who left their houses in Beit Lahia and Beit Hanoun and returned to the UNRWA school for shelter, like my cousins. They

---

* Hanaa Naim Balata, Doaa Naim Balata, Israa Naim Balata, Mariam Naim Balata, Yehya Naim Balata, Naim Nathmi, and Sahar Motawea Balata (ages unknown) were all killed in the same attack.

did not die or get injured in their homes, which continue to stand untouched in the crossfire, rather in the safest place they knew, in a UN building.

It is a game of luck that you have no hand in. Today, as I prepare an espresso, looking down from the window of my kitchen, I realize that this longing for the taste of espresso, or my yearning for my desk back in my study, might be part of a scene in the final act of a story. Every action you take, every small gesture, might be part of your final act. The coffee is boiling as I look down from my window, and I ask myself: What if an F16 pilot does not like the smudge my coffee makes on his infrared screen, watching my house; what if the operator of a drone hovering over my building is annoyed by the steam coming from the coffee maker, steaming up the window, and therefore his view into my house on his computer screen somewhere in Israel? What if the pilot in the aircraft is in a bad mood generally this morning and doesn't mind pressing the button on a whim, seeing steam fog up my window, thinking that will do as a reason? He might have quarreled with his girlfriend this morning or didn't manage to have sex with her last night . . . and I have to pay for this.

More than half of my coffee has boiled over onto the stove before I return from my reverie. I can't help having such thoughts. The sound of explosions, the whir of drones, the hissing of warships' shells, the wail of ambulances, the cries of people in the street, and the worry I see in the eyes of my wife and kids . . . all these make me think of the moment when all my savings in the bank of luck will be spent. That moment will come without pre-notification. I can't check my balance. It will just happen. Making a simple cup of coffee might put me in the red, or listening to the radio in the middle of the night, or sitting in front of the building with my neighbors, or walking to my father's place, or having a nargilah with my friends. Anything could potentially drain the last penny of credit from my account. I might be a danger to others too. I might be an omen for someone else's bad luck, for all I know.

Come evening, I order a taxi to take Mostafa to stay at his grandfather's house as I need to take him to al-Awda Hospital early in the morning to have a minor operation on his arm. When we near the Falouja area of the camp, an explosion suddenly flashes in front of us, deafening me for a moment. I watch as shrapnel sprays up into the sky in front of us. The driver responds instantly, putting the car in reverse and speeding back down the street. A spray of shrapnel, stone, and brick seems to darken the sky in front us, like a rain cloud or an oncoming storm. Then it all crashes down, just a few meters in front of us. Any one of these pieces could have killed us had it struck the car.

I phone my friend Hisham. He has just returned home from work in Beit Hanoun Hospital. His family is all spread out over the Strip these days. He and his wife are staying in their house in Beit Hanoun. His married sons are staying with their fathers-in-law while his other children are staying at a relative's. He says this is a good way to prevent the whole family from being killed by a single strike: "Some of us will survive if one of the places gets hit," he says. I suggest that Hisham and his wife come and stay with me in my place since it's safer than their house in Beit Hanoun. "Nowhere in Gaza is safer than anywhere else," he replies. "It's all dangerous." It's the same logic that drove my cousins, after the strike on their UNRWA shelter, to return to their home in north Beit Lahia. It's all the same.

After forty-seven days of continued attacks and the unbearable burden of trying to survive, it doesn't matter. You don't live by choice, just as you don't die by choice.

Jabalia Camp

ZAFIR FOUR

I RISE EARLY TO take Mostafa to the hospital. By 7 a.m., we are standing in the lobby of al-Awda Hospital in Tel Azaatar, accompanied by my father-in-law, who shares his first name with Mostafa. Everything is calm and quiet. There were few explosions during the night, only the occasional sound of a drone or an F16 breaking the sound barrier. The usual morning questions—Where did the latest attacks take place? How many have been killed?—are beginning to subside under the weight of everyday life. It's not that that these questions don't matter anymore, it's rather that they have become quite ordinary. Other, everyday topics of conversation compete with them.

After an hour's examination and preparation, Mostafa is taken through to the operating theater. It's a routine operation, quite straightforward. After twenty minutes, the nurse brings him back in a wheelchair. He's fully conscious; only a local anesthetic. Everything's fine, the nurse tells me, with a tired, pale smile. We have to wait for two hours before we can take Mostafa home. I feel a bit guilty being there, taking up the doctor's and surgeon's time with a simple lipoma in my son's arm while others lie maimed, mutilated, and dying elsewhere in the hospital. My son said he could no longer take the pain three days ago, so I had to book him in for this. At first, I told him we can wait until the war stops but, by the next day, he couldn't move his fingers properly as the lipoma was on the main artery in his arm and affecting his tendons. I remember the look in the eyes of the pharmacist at al-Nasser Hospital, two days ago, when I took her a prescription. She was painting her nails and didn't look like she'd got out of her chair all day. Now I realize how surprised she must have been at someone asking for eye drops for a child when other children were losing their heads.

I imagine that all of Gaza is sick right now. Everyone must be suffering with something. But, as the hospitals are on full alert, people don't feel comfortable complaining about a simple chest infection or mere aches and pains, even though they could be symptoms of more serious things. If people don't get treatment for straightforward ailments, the whole country will run the risk of getting even sicker.

It's a well-documented fact that the number of cases of cancer in Gaza has risen significantly over the last five years.[1] One of the many hypotheses suggested is the extensive use of white phosphorus by the Israeli army in its weapons during the war on Gaza in December 2008 and January 2009. Several acquaintances of mine were diagnosed with cancer in the months that followed and some didn't even have time to get treatment, it was so far progressed. In Gaza there is no proper treatment for these people. Instead they have to seek treatment in Israel, Egypt, or Jordan, and with the blockade imposed on Gaza since 2007, very few have the right connections to get a permit to leave through these largely closed borders.

Later, near my home, I bump into Moeen—the guy who I've been buying grapes and figs from all summer. He confides that this evening was meant to be the night of his oldest son's wedding party. "I had to cancel it." Moeen usually sets out his fresh fruit in boxes, arranged in front of the UNRWA girls' school on Makbara Street. He sits himself on one of the empty plastic crates and smokes nargilah while his son looks after the customers. "Man, I can't have a party while people are dying. . . . Five of my relatives were killed four weeks ago. Never mind about my neighbors and friends." I understand what he says and ask why he doesn't go ahead with the wedding without the party. He draws on the nargilah and exhales heavy clouds of smoke into the summer afternoon. "Are you crazy? This is my first kid to get married. I want to feel happy. I want to celebrate." So his son will have to wait a few more months.

Moeen asks, "What if the war never ends? I mean, it's into its second month; maybe they plan to just keep going?"

This time I have to give him hope. "Don't worry," I say. "It will end."

He smiles. "I know. It has to someday. But I want it to end soon so that I can celebrate my son's wedding." He puts more coke on the top of the tobacco. "You never know. The war is like fire"— pointing at the coke—"it eats everything."

I take the grapes and figs that he's prepared for me and remind him to invite me to the wedding party, whenever it is. He smiles and says, "You'll be the first on the list." As I walk away I shout back to him that there are only two weeks left of the season for grapes, so I will remember to buy his as often as possible before the end of the season. He doesn't need to advertise his goods; he doesn't need to tell me that his fruit is the best. I've been buying from him for seven years.

This evening, news reaches us that an F16 has destroyed the Zafir Four Tower in Tel al-Hawa.[2] This is one of Gaza's most beautiful buildings, boasting fourteen floors and forty-five apartments. Or rather it was. A small rocket struck the roof of the tower first, forcing everyone to evacuate and pour out onto the street. A few minutes later, two more rockets struck, and the tower came down. One of these rockets hit one of the main support pillars so the whole thing collapsed sideways. For hours, flames engulfed the rubble, devouring smashed furniture, clothes, family heirlooms, cherished personal belongings.

More than 320 people were left without a place to sleep. My friend Hisham Saqallah, a journalist and blogger who barely made it out of the building in time in his wheelchair, wrote immediately on his Facebook wall, describing the devastation of his dream flat. All the surrounding towers were damaged by the blast as well. A friend of mine in a neighboring building found flames jumping into her room through the window. Besides the residents of Zafir Four, hundreds of others had to evacuate their flats in the building adjacent to it as the damage had rendered it unsafe as well. In the hours that follow, I hear scores of stories from different friends about it.

As the stories pile up, Hanna becomes more nervous about our own building. I try to calm her. There's no logic to it. Just because an F16 hits a modern tower like Zafir Four, doesn't mean it will target other modern residences in the Strip like ours. I explain to her that our building is only five floors high; it's not a tower. She smiles and asks, "What is the difference? It's not about the difference. It's about the non-logic of war!"

I try to argue that there must be a reason for destroying a fourteen-storey building and leaving more than 320 people homeless. And whatever it is, it doesn't apply to our little block. But later, alone, I realize her argument makes sense.

Sunday, 24 August

DRESSING FOR
THE WORST

IT'S EARLY AFTERNOON, and we have no food in for lunch. I
leave the apartment and head for the souq in Sheikh Radwan to get
a couple of chickens and vegetables. I walk south along Ahmad Yassen Street for about fifteen minutes, and I'm about halfway down
it when three missiles suddenly hit the street behind me. The explosion sends flames high into the air like angry hands reaching
up to the sky. I can't work out the exact target. It might be close to
our building; it's hard to judge the distance. I dial Hanna's mobile;
she doesn't answer. I start to panic, then try to calm myself. She's
probably left her mobile in the other room. The attacks can't be on
our building. It looks closer. The flames quickly die down. Somehow, I know if it was our building, they'd be raging for hours. I try
the house number a couple of times. On the third attempt Hanna
answers. She sounds as panicked as me. She thought that the attacks might have struck me. We're both equally lucky to be wrong.

She insists that I come back. "What will we eat then?"

"We don't need to eat!"

I make my way to the Sheikh Radwan souq all the same and
buy the chickens and vegetables before heading back the same way
I came. It's very hot. All the way back, I try to walk in the shade of
the trees and houses on the left-hand side of the street. I know I

shouldn't do this. War teaches you to always walk in the middle of the street, to minimize the risk of being hit by shrapnel or debris if one of the buildings on either side is hit. Likewise, whenever you see a car or motorcycle come down the street, steer well clear. Put a minimum of twenty feet, if you can, between you and the vehicle. Vehicles are a moving target. You don't have to be.

When I get home, Hanna criticizes me for wanting to put on shorts. She tells me I should always be fully dressed. She herself hasn't worn shorts or a nightdress for over a month: "We need to be ready to evacuate quickly, at any moment, and what we're wearing might be all we have. Also, if we're injured, at least we will look respectable when we're taken to the hospital."

I tell her it's all the same. We won't feel anything and no one else will care if we're naked or fully dressed. She twitches, refusing to accept this. "You never know what is going to happen," she says. "We may have to live on the street, or run to a different part of the city, or move to a hospital or a school." I laugh at this idea but know inside that she has a point. It seems war dictates what we wear as well.

I suggest to Hanna that she stop listening to the news. Each time she turns on the radio, she becomes obsessed with the idea of the apartment being hit or losing one of the kids. Our life is the news, I tell her, so there's no point getting even more frustrated or disappointed by searching for new news. My point is, when you listen to the radio, you get the feeling everything is slowly collapsing around you. Each time you hear of a loss of life somewhere else in the Strip, your mind calculates the distance between there and here; you picture a map of the Strip with the latest target and the next one—you. The numbers of the dead, the screams of the injured, the cries of their families—these all make up the soundtrack to this map, which has an X over your apartment.

Every moment, there is breaking news. If you want to follow it properly, you can't really afford to do anything except follow it. My friends from Beit Hanoun, currently sheltering in the UNRWA school opposite, are even more addicted to it than Hanna. I go to see two of them this evening—Abu Basil and Ibrahim—and they don't stop talking for one moment about what the news said about this or what the news said about that. The two of them know the position of every politician, country, and party involved in the Cairo talks. I can understand why: it dictates every minute detail of their lives. They want the news to tell them that the war is going to end in an hour's time, or ten minutes' time, or better still that it has ended already.

The news is about them—about the refugees in the schools, the loss of homes—it tells them nothing but what they already know, better than anyone else. But still they follow it. They want to be surprised, to learn that they've been ignorant all along of some key aspect of what's happening around them. Ibrahim wants to hear good news so he can return to his house again and get his bathroom back. During the last five-day truce, a few refugees whose houses weren't damaged returned to them briefly. Ibrahim was one of them. For five days, he slept in his own bed, took showers and had the privacy of his bathroom. He tries to explain the joy of getting his bathroom back. In the UNRWA school, when you use the bathroom, you know there are three dozen people queuing outside, waiting for you to finish. They let you know about it.

I try to tell them both they shouldn't be listening to the radio for good news. When it comes, you don't need the radio to hear it. You hear it from the street; good news knocks on your door. It enters through the window like a cool breeze or a swarm of butterflies.

In the evening, my father comes to see Mostafa after his operation. It's hot in the room. He plays with the kids for an hour or so and then decides to head back. Mostafa and Talal want to go with him. It's been over a week since they've played their blessed PlayStations in the Internet cafés near my father's house. He asks me if they can. The four of us take a taxi there, and Mostafa and Talal persuade me to give them two hours in the Internet café before they have to go to my father's.

After I drop them off, I go to my friend Faraj's place. The whole neighborhood is in pitch darkness. Electricity hasn't returned here for thirty hours. A shell strike to the north of Gaza means this area has been cut off longer than others. I can't bear to sit for more than half an hour with Faraj and Abu Aseel, so I give my apologies and walk home. It's now 10 p.m. and, to me, the whole city seems asleep.

THE WAR ON BEAUTY

WHENEVER I WALK through the city at night, I keep one eye firmly fixed on the sky. Against the dark blue of an August night, a drone looks like any other star, glinting from its random position in the firmament. I know that at least one drone is always up there, hiding among the constellations. I search for it. After a few seconds, I can usually spot one—a tiny light, swimming through the dark blue sea above my head. I train my eye on it and nothing else. I tell myself that I have to look this monster in the eye if I'm to see when he fires a missile at me. I have to see the missile as it drops out of the undercarriage of the thing. It takes a few seconds to reach me, so that's how long I have to get out of there. Initially, I thought the best course of action would be to run under a tree and hope its branches would absorb some of the impact. Then I thought about running in the opposite direction, down the street. Whatever I do, right now I just have to be vigilant of any slight movement the drone makes. I have to watch it as it watches me. I have to concentrate not to lose it to the darkness. I don't want to be lost to the darkness either. As it hovers above me, I spot another over to my right, then a third one on the left and a fourth one behind me. I am surrounded by a squadron of drones. I can't help but imagine that they have just one plan: to kill me. They're arguing over who's going to have the first shot. If I run, I will look more like a reasonable target, a dangerous threat in motion.

I keep walking steadily, changing the side of the street I walk on from time to time. When I near a particular house, I tell myself, "This house will definitely be targeted, or the one beside it." So I cross over to the other side of the street before realizing how stupid this is; any house, on either side of the street, might be targeted. It occurs to me that walking erratically like this, from side to side, may draw the attention of the drone operator. He might suspect that I am trying to avoid being seen, that I have something to hide. It is better to be obvious, I realize, so I opt for my old tactic and walk straight down the middle of the street. This way the drone operator sees me perfectly clearly; he knows I have nothing to hide. Then I ask myself, what if a car speeds down the street behind me in the dark? I might not hear him or get out of the way in time. Or worse, what if the car is targeted just as it approaches me? These are the kind of thoughts that make a Gazan walk a little faster at night.

The Israelis are carefully removing any beauty the city has left. So far, they have targeted every modern building, every attractive piece of architecture. Not only do they want to make the people look ugly— ugly in our grief—they want to make Gaza look ugly too. They want nothing to be left but a gray, rubble-strewn slum. Tonight, the radio announces that a drone has fired four small missiles into the Italian Complex. The Israeli army has declared its intention to destroy the entire complex, which contains a fifteen-storey residential tower, a shopping center, and many beautifully adorned cafés. My friends and I used to visit these cafés a lot, especially back when I was living right beside the complex a few years ago.

They tell us pointedly that they are going to keep bombing this complex until there's nothing left, knowing full well how much it is cherished in Gaza as one of the city's most beautiful buildings. Before the war ends, they don't want to miss this opportunity to erase something we all love. Watch carefully, they're saying. See how gradually it falls, one piece at a time, as we bomb it live on television.

I sit in front of the TV with Hanna, watching dutifully. There's a live view of the Italian Complex, which is shrouded in darkness between each strike. I look up at the window on the south side of the apartment facing al-Nasser, where the complex is situated. I can see the flash of the missiles lighting up the glass—each flash on the glass about half a second ahead of the flash on the TV. I get up and go to the window for a better, untelevised view. As soon as I get there, a huge explosion shakes the building. I check Facebook to see what people are saying. Another explosion. The missiles continue to eat away at us like rot within an apple; sadness continues to coagulate in our hearts. The TV presenter tells us that missiles are hitting the complex from all sides, but it's still standing.

Hanna and I follow the tower's slow death like watching a martyrdom unfolding. I sit exhausted on the blue sofa, listening to a choir of voices from both the TV and the radio. When a missile lights up the glass of the window, I jump up to see if I can trace the origin of the missile, work out which side's been hit. The building shakes to the right and left. The sound of the reporter's panting as he runs for cover fills my ears. The susurration of the wind sounds like the lament of women stumbling in the road.

They are stripping the city of its beauty. They want to make us ugly, to drag us from the clean spring to the polluted water downstream. The Italian Complex has now entered the past. The lovely café at the base of the tower is gone. The spacious, flowered gardens I used to sit in have now said their farewell to this anxious city. The wooden tables and chairs, the nargilah pipes that would fly off the shelves of the cafés, have all blown away. No evidence remains to support our memories of the place. The evidence of my conversation with my friend Ramzi, two weeks ago, sitting at one of the tables, has fallen onto the wet grass of the garden and been buried under the dust and rubble. Unfinished thoughts shared with friends over a nargilah have now blown away with the smoke and flames that followed the attack.

The Italian Complex was erased just as the Zafir Four Tower was. All the best buildings are now in ruins, flattened or, if standing, flayed with sides missing, windows blown out, structurally unsound. The drone operator must have been annoyed to see these small patches of beauty that Gaza had created. Perhaps he was surprised that Gaza could ever have blossomed like this, like a girl blossoming into womanhood. He wanted to uproot its femininity.

As we watch the last shards of the Italian Complex crash down, we hear news of another F16 attack on al-Basha Tower at the end of al-Jala'a Street. Al-Basha was one of the first tall buildings to be erected in Gaza. The Ministry of Culture set up its very first office there in 1994. It had a couple of rooms in the tower before moving to a different building. The Al-Basha site remains the home of many key cultural organizations and artists to this day. The Gaza Institute for Art and Culture is based there. An artist and friend of mine, Majdal Nateel, has her studio there. Many other artists have studios there, including Iyad Sabah and the film director Khalil Mozain. The radio station Sha'ab is also located in the tower, one of the few non-Islamist radio stations in Gaza. In those studios and offices, I have shared so many coffees and had so many great debates—agreeing with many, disagreeing with many others. I remember my first steps up the stairs of the tower in August 1995. I was twenty-two years old at the time and in my last year at university. I was going to see the then director general of the Ministry of Culture, Ahmad Dahbour, one of the greatest living Palestinian poets.[1] I knew Dahbour's work from my studies. His poem "The Palestinian Boy" is one that all students learn by heart. I wanted to show him what I was writing, some samples of my short fiction. I remember my nervousness as I knocked on his door. I'm very proud to say we became good friends and remained close, until he eventually decided to leave Gaza, like so many writers. Now his offices have gone as well.

THIS IS THE DAY

THE WAR HAS ENDED. And so far . . . it's not a joke! Sometimes miracles happen, and, when they do, they broadcast their own news, tell their own story. Thousands of people are in the streets celebrating. You can hear someone firing a rifle into the air. Cars are speeding up and down the streets, filling the air with their horns. Boys are riding motorcycles, trailing flags behind them. Women are standing on balconies and doorsteps watching the festivities. Old men have brought bamboo chairs out into the street to sit and watch the proceedings while smoking tobacco. The smell of it spreads through the street. The leaves of the jasmine tree climbing up the side of my neighbor's house flutter joyfully in the breeze coming in from the west. Everything is joyous. A bazaar of sounds!

In a moment, everything changed. Up until an hour ago, all evidence pointed to the war continuing for weeks. There had been coverage of the Cairo negotiations all day, as well as intimations that a permanent cease-fire was on the cards, but such intimations have been made for weeks. Most commentators were skeptical. Hanna had been listening to the news since mid-afternoon. One report suggested there would be some kind of breakthrough by 7 p.m. "This might be it!" she suggested. But nothing in the city backed it up. The drones were still hovering; explosions could still be heard a few miles off. I honestly expected it to be yet another joke of Middle East politics. She chided me: "This is not another joke. This time it's different."

The radio announced that President Abbas was going to address the nation at 7 p.m. Commentators suggested he would announce that the Palestinian delegation in Cairo had accepted the Egyptian proposal for a cease-fire. Over the last few days, negotiations had focused on four issues: the rebuilding of Gaza's international airport; the building of a seaport or harbor; the opening of the Rafah border point with Egypt, which has been closed for the best part of a year; and the means by which to reconstruct the thousands of buildings destroyed by the war. Each one of these was an attempt to end or mitigate the siege that Israel has imposed on the Strip for more than eight years. The idea of an airport was the most ambitious of these; the brief period when Gazans could fly freely to anywhere in the world from their own airport is like a fairytale to most of us rather than a period of history. I'll never forget the day the first Palestinian aircraft flew from that airport. It was 23 November 1998. At the time, I was in England, studying at the University of Bradford. Like most Palestinians, I spent hours watching joyful TV images of a country that had waited fifty years to have its own airport! In October 2000, the Israelis bombed the airstrip into rubble; nothing but weeds has grown there since.

It's difficult for people in the West to really appreciate how lucky they are to be able to travel freely and without humiliation through checkpoints and borders. No one appreciates the value of this freedom more than Palestinians. Hanna asks me if I think there will really be an airport one day. Mostafa says he would prefer a seaport. He would love to travel by sea. Never has there been an entire land of people, living by and partly off the sea, who have been unable to ever really go to sea—yet another paradox of Gaza.[1]

Then suddenly, in the middle of these idle speculations, there is the realization that we wouldn't be having these conversations if this time was the same as all the others. The TV presenter is suddenly full of confidence, declaring that a new dawn was coming for Gaza: a time when the Strip would be free again with an airport and a seaport, with free movement through the Rafah crossing, freedom to travel and worship in Jerusalem, when construction material would be imported un-rationed, when all goods and all people would move freely. The smile on his face as he says all this is as wide as the TV screen.

It is getting close to 7 p.m. and we can still hear occasional explosions across the city. The drone operator isn't following the TV the way we are. Or he wants to make the most of his last go at the game, for now.

Facebook is full of friends posting little snippets that they've heard about the deal soon to be announced in Cairo. Bit by bit, the end of the war becomes more real. Then more good news—independent of the news or social media: the mosques believe the war has ended too. Their own singers are calling in celebration with loud-hailers, from the minarets and down in the streets as well.

I say to Hanna: "We made it. We've survived." We've lived through fifty-one days that felt more like fifty-one months. The only good thing about war, when you realize you've survived it, is that it is in the past, finally. It's over. Even though you can still smell its stench in the streets, you can still see the shadows of it on the walls of the city, in the gaps where buildings used to be. But you've made it! To think, only a few minutes ago you weren't sure if you were going to live or die in this war. Now suddenly it's over.

The street below our balcony is full of people gathering in front of the shops on the other side. People are frantically exchanging theories and interpretations of the news. The callers from the mosques celebrate by reminding us of the promise of God, every so often reciting excerpts from the Koran. All the mosques in Gaza are now doing the same. A militia man gives another speech from a car that roams the streets. Boys are starting to set off fireworks. No need now for the radio, TV, or Facebook. Now the news is spreading physically through the streets.

During the last fifty-one days, I've occasionally doubted if I was actually still alive and wondered if those around me—Hanna and the kids—were in fact all dead as well. I've wondered if we all occupied a kind of limbo instead, with the real war and the real world carrying on in the background. Maybe we were all killed in a drone attack in the first week of the war? Sometimes, the dead visit the living and participate in their lives without the living noticing it. This is what my grandmother Aisha used to say. For the last fifty-one days, I haven't been sure which part I've been playing.

It was a nightmare. You can add any adjective you like in front of this word—a terrifying nightmare, a surreal nightmare—but the worst of it is that it's not actually a nightmare at all. It doesn't end. Sometimes you want to hit your head against a wall just to see if it will wake you up. One night, I remember lying in bed, unable to sleep for the sound of the explosions. I suddenly had the urge to jam my fingers into the electrical socket to see if I was actually dreaming. To see what the shock would do. I nearly did. It was only the next explosion that stopped me, making me jump up to the window, as usual, to see what had happened, to stare into the darkness and wish once more that I was dreaming.

Now the border between sleep and wakefulness sharpens back into focus. It is real—these fireworks I hear whizzing into the air. It is true—these joyous colors I can see blooming into the sky above me! It is actual—these celebrations taking place!

From my balcony, I can see thousands of people heading in the direction of Saftawi Square to celebrate. People are hugging each other. Boys are setting off firecrackers. Flags are being brandished at the sky as if to tease the drone that still hovers up there. I know that, down amongst them, the younger people will already be dreaming about travel: seeing the world that has been denied them for so much of their lives so far. Also, from my balcony, I can just about make out the boughs of the old sycamore tree, still standing just as it always was, reminding me, once more, that I've survived.

My kids are overjoyed. Each one asks me the same question in different ways: Is this really the end of it? Without waiting for my answer, the boys run out into the street, leaving little Jaffa crying and wanting to follow them, slamming the door behind them. She shrieks like never before, as if she knows that she is missing the most joyful moment in her young life. The moment we all realize she has survived. After a few minutes, she acquiesces and goes out onto the balcony, wanting to watch and hear the world celebrating outside, wanting to still be part of it. But she struggles to see over the edge of the balcony. Then suddenly she smiles; above us fireworks are decorating the sky with color. She laughs and points at them: "Doooooooooor!" she says. Then she jumps up clinging to my legs. I pick her up so she has a better view; she is so excited by the new world she is living in now.

Can you believe today is also our wedding anniversary? I never forget the date, but this year, if the war had continued, it would have eaten into the happiness of the occasion. Now, it is simply a great day.

We woke this morning to the sound of mortar shelling. I muttered to Hanna, through the haze of sleep, that the machines of war were serenading us the way we were serenaded on our wedding day. I made out a smile flickering across her face—the same smile she had on our very first date together when we met in that café on the beach. But today, the smile doesn't linger very long. Dread and anxiety return to her expression; this was no time for celebration.

I tell Hanna: "Remember the twenty-sixth of August is always a happy day."

It was true. Now everyone is celebrating in the street; everyone is happy. Hanna is happy, the boys are happy. Moments like this will come to an end; happiness may betray you later down the line,

I know this. But hope never betrays you. It is there when you need it; you just have to believe in it and keep it safe inside. You must never give it up.

The war ended. Which of us could have predicted that we were going to live to see this day? What logic could have calculated this? Only hope.

One thing we need to do, I tell Salim and Aed over the phone, shouting to be heard above the noise of the celebrations, is to go to al-Samra Hamam, the bathhouse, to wash our bodies from all the smells of war. Usually, we would go in the early evening around 5:30 p.m., when no one else is there, and talk through the steam of the medieval *hamam*. My father goes to the *hamam* every Eid before the Eid prayers, leaving the house well before dawn.

Now it is over.

Thinking of what to do tomorrow is better than dwelling on the pain of yesterday. It was hard. It was terrible. But it was not us who created that hell. The only thing we can create is tomorrow.

It is over now. I need to sleep and dream of nothing at all. Just lie in the dark and leave all images and noises to one side. I want to look into the face of little Jaffa and be able to promise her a future free of the fear of being killed. I want to see the boys playing in the street without danger. I want to return to the fine details of my everyday life: to go to the café with friends, to read a book quietly in silence, to sit up late watching a movie with Hanna, to wake up in the morning not thinking, "Who has survived the night?"

Now I can eat alone with no drone watching over me. No longer will I have the pilot of an F16, or the captain of a warship out at sea, or soldiers huddled in a tank two miles away, or the drone operator sitting at a desk in Israel, or Netanyahu, eating with me. For the first time in fifty-one days, I will eat, drink, think, sleep, and take a shower alone, with nobody else there. The air will be all mine and I will breathe it.

AFTERWORD

IT'S BEEN NEARLY six months since the war ended, and reading over this diary now, my first instinct is to feel a little foolish about the hopes expressed on the last day of the war. For many thousands of Gazans, the suffering continues and the promises seem to have all been broken.[1] The war ended, officially, on 26 August, but for those who were left homeless or bereaved, or with their livelihoods destroyed, the war goes on. The only difference is the world isn't watching anymore.[2]

Thousands of Gazans are still living in the UNRWA schools, converted during the war into emergency refugee centers,[3] which means other schools have to accommodate twice as many pupils in their classrooms. In December, I visited one of these makeshift-but-abiding refugee centers in Beit Hanoun and the images I took from it were straight out of the war itself: washing hanging from every window, classrooms heaving with displaced families, girls queuing patiently in front of the water tank in the playground. You can see the strain and worry in people's eyes. Gazans are not haunted by the past, or by grief, as much as they are haunted by the future, the uncertainty of whether they will cope.

The rebuilding has barely begun. You see the devastation lying untouched, everywhere. Sometimes I have the feeling that we are all so inured to this kind of destruction, another war would make no difference. We're used to losing everything. We try to grab what little moments of pleasure we can from life but most of the time it doesn't happen. My son Mostafa asked me the other day: "Daddy, when will the next war be?" He is eleven years old and has witnessed three wars in his short life; already he's planning for the fourth.

Now all the conversations in the souq focus on cement—when once it might have been the date of the next truce, or the negotiations taking place in Cairo. When will the shipments of concrete reach Gaza? When will the other construction material be allowed in?[4] My friend Abu Annas always jokes at these speculations, saying Gaza should indulge in another war in which our main demand is cement.

My friend Tarik lost his four-storey house in the summer and is fed up with waiting for the construction material to arrive so he can start rebuilding. The sight every morning of his life's savings flattened into rubble has dragged him into depression. For more than three months, he waited for government assistance before eventually giving up and starting the long process of removing the rubble and rebuilding his house, singlehandedly, at his own expense. Rent prices in Gaza City have gone sky-high to match the demand for places to live. Some people are exploiting the situation, moving in with relatives and renting out their own homes at astronomic rates. No one is controlling the situation.

My farmer friend Nafiz now lives in my flat in the Nasser quarter, while he waits for construction material to arrive for his farmhouse's reconstruction. Every morning he goes to East Beit Hanoun to follow up on some detail or another related to the delay. He tells me that when he listens to the latest update, he barely understands a word about the bureaucracy of applying for materials and the logistics of the purchase and delivery. He says: "All I want to do is rebuild my house. I don't care about the rest of it!"

Hisham, the hospital clerk, has started to repair his house in the Masreen district of Beit Hanoun. He has fit new windows and doors and started to rebuild his kitchen on the side of the house that was hit. It's enough, at least, to let him move back in. His attitude is one of gratitude: "We're luckier than others," he says. "At least we have a place to sleep." When I visited him two weeks ago, we all sat around the stove in front of his house. Hisham was reluctantly stoking the fire with wood from the olive, orange, and peach trees that had been uprooted by Israeli bulldozers around his house. Most of us felt the warmth of the stove appreciatively on that cold January evening. Hisham did not.

Political quarrels between Ramallah and Gaza only add insult to injury. The people suffering in Gaza right now need assistance, nothing else. They don't care about the rights and wrongs, the political point-scoring, or what party's name is attached to the help; all that matters is that they get help.

A Swedish journalist asked me a week after the war ended, "Who do you think won the war?"

I replied: "I did. I won it by surviving." But when I think back to those fifty-one days of bombardment, I see that the war's darkest spots of horror and panic still have a hold on me. For several weeks after the cease-fire, I felt like I was still in the middle of it. Like most people, I felt drugged by the closeness of death and still suffer the occasional, dizzying flashback.

In January, a group of young artists led by Dalia Abdel-Rahman gathered at Gaza's harbor to paint the blocks in the walls along the quay different colors. These walls are only a few blocks high and the water in which the fishermen moor their boats is just a few feet deep. When I spoke to Dalia on a recent visit to the Tamer Institute, where she works, she explained that painting these blocks in bright colors was their way of making progress, of giving the fishermen (and Gazans generally) a sense that things are genuinely moving forward.

Since this first explosion of color, others have started to write words and phrases on the blocks, just as Palestinians in the West

Bank have graffitied the Separation Wall. Phrases like "Free Gaza," "I Choose You, My Country," and "I Call On You"[5] now decorate the multi-colored harbor wall. Thanks to the graffiti, this humble, slightly haphazard wall has joined the far uglier, towering Separation Wall built by the Israelis as an instrument of imprisonment. Yesterday, I took Hanna and the children to check the progress of this unfolding artwork. (I should explain that the port doubles as a public park of sorts; for most Gazans it's one of the nicest places to meet and relax.) As we were looking at the graffiti, I suggested to Hanna that the Pope should come to Gaza and pray at this wall, just as he did at the Separation Wall near Bethlehem in May last year. She laughed: "Yes, we were a bit jealous." The kids always enjoyed spending time at the port, although I can never answer Naeem very accurately when he points out to sea and asks how far towards the horizon, exactly, we are allowed to sail.[6]

Due to the plummeting fish stocks within the restriction zone, many fishermen make their money offering short trips around the quays. This has combined with Dalia's initiative to make visiting the port like going to a gallery, where you see the work by boat.

No such ingenuity has been applied so far to the disused Gaza airport. I remember when I was about six years old and my father went to work in Saudi Arabia for a few months. Whenever I asked my mother when he'd be back, she would say: "Look up to the sky. If you see a plane, it might be him." I used to scour the Gazan sky every morning searching for his plane. Now, only F16s and drones can be seen up there. Grass grows over the cracks in the runway. Not once have I been able to take a plane from Gaza. No Gazans of my generation, or younger, have. The way things are going they never will.

Saed Lolo, an activist in the 15 March Youth Coalition and one of the leaders of the huge demonstration in Gaza in 2011 that called for an end to the Fatah-Hamas infighting, organized a demonstration in Shuja'iyya on 7 January with his comrades to support the people who lost their houses in the war. Saed and his comrades gathered on Nazaz Street in the Shuja'iyya quarter wearing only boxer shorts and vests. It was freezing and raining mercilessly. Afterwards, in the Karawan Café, he was shivering from the cold, but saying it was nothing compared to what thousands of Gazans faced this winter: "Why isn't anything being done to help these people?" he asked, his teeth still chattering. "They've had to live without homes for five months now! Nobody seems to care!"

Looking at this diary, I feel foolish about other things too, like the daily rituals I maintained. Why, for instance, did I risk my life every day walking to and from the Internet café just to type these pages? I guess you have to be foolish to survive the madness. I certainly was.

Four days ago, the government erected two signs by the harbor wall: one reads "Arrival Quay," the other "Departure Quay."[7] Friends have already posted a Photoshopped image of the former sign on Facebook, showing *Titanic* pulling into the harbor behind it. Another Facebook friend wrote on his wall, "Breaking news: a date for opening of the port and Rafah crossing has been set. . . . Doomsday!"

However ludicrous the "Departure" and "Arrival" signs may look, standing there at the quayside with nothing but a handful of tiny wooden fishing boats in the background, they act as symbols; they attempt to do what Dalia did so beautifully a few weeks before: show progress. For my family, walking along the quay yesterday, they also pointed to an undeniable fact: the existence of a world beyond the sea, a world that the single word "Departure" aspires to reach.

—*Gaza, February 2015*

EDITOR'S NOTE
TO THE UK EDITION

THIS BOOK WASN'T supposed to happen. It grew out of an earlier publication that was in many ways its exact opposite.

In June 2014, Comma Press launched an anthology of short stories by Gazan writers, edited by Atef Abu Saif, titled *The Book of Gaza*, as part of our City in Short Fiction series. We planned to bring two authors over to the UK for launch events: Atef himself and Abdallah Tayeh. Due to the Rafah border with Egypt remaining closed in the immediate aftermath of the Egyptian election, only Atef was able to make it out (via the Erez border), and he appeared at well-attended events in London, Manchester, Liverpool, and Hay-on-Wye.

The anthology had two explicit aims: to give a platform to the city's writing, just as platforms are given to other cities' literature; and to present an alternative picture of Gaza for the reader, one devoid of the usual political rhetoric and atrocity-porn that pervades the media's portrait of the Strip. We're all familiar with the basic vocabulary of this war-porn: the bomb-damaged buildings, the hysterical mourners, the angry funeral processions, the suited Hamas/Israeli spokesmen standing behind banks of microphones—images that are both extremely familiar and utterly impossible to connect to. *The Book of Gaza* strove to bring the normal life of Gazans into the foreground for a change, to spotlight the domestic, the ordinary, and the everyday—human stories that Gaza, like any other city, must be teeming with. In short, it strove to depoliticize Gaza.

On 12 June, the very day Atef returned from his UK tour, three Israeli teenagers—Naftali Fraenkel, Gilad Shaer, and Eyal Yifrah—were kidnapped and later murdered by a "lone cell"[1] of Palestinian extremists in the West Bank. Four weeks later, Israel launched perhaps its most brutal onslaught on the Gazan people in decades, as an apparent response to this tragedy. Even according to Israel's own narrative for how the war came about, the attack was a collective punishment of an entire people for having voted in Hamas (a party Israel claimed had sanctioned the teenagers' murders). Of course, there was far more to it than that one tragedy.

With the first wave of attacks, the very authors we had worked with for several months were suddenly fearing for their lives. Watching the nightly news, we felt as helpless as everyone else across the world. The bombardment was relentless, the targeting barbaric. As an editor, I thought I'd gotten to know the Strip a little, vicariously, through the stories, but quickly Gaza was being restored to its former state: a mere target for another country's venom; a city-wide pile of rubble; a setting for yet another angry, seemingly endless Palestinian funeral procession.

I Facebooked and Whatsapped the contributors whenever I saw they were online, and although moved by their replies, didn't exactly know what to do with them, other than re-post them on my own Facebook wall.[2] What we all hoped would last just a week or so took fifty-one merciless days. Asmaa al-Ghoul, one of the contributors to the anthology, lost nine members of her extended family in Rafah on 3 August (p. 149). Mohammed Ghalayini, a Manchester-based consultant who had helped Comma with *The Book of Gaza*, lost nine members of his extended family in Khan Younis on 1 August.[*] Atef lost his stepbrother.

---

[*] Abdel-Malek Abdel-Salaam El-Farra (fifty-four), Emaad Abdel-Hafiz El-Farra (twenty-eight), Osama Abdel-Malek El-Farra (thirty-four), Awatef Izzidin El-Farra (twenty-nine), Mohammed Mahmoud El-Farra (twelve), Lujain Basem El-Farra (four), Yara Abdel-Salaam El-Farra (eight), Nadine Mahmoud El-Farra (eight), and Abdel-Rahman Yassir Abdel-Malek El-Farra (eight).

For many days in mid-July, I could do nothing but offer my solidarity to those writers caught in the middle of it. I urged them to keep writing, to keep paying witness to what was happening to their city, as any editor might. But I couldn't claim to know what, if anything, would come of their writing. Very quickly, though, the authors' messages that I'd shared on Facebook began to be re-posted, in turn, by other friends and then picked up by bloggers (especially readers who'd attended Atef's events just a few weeks before). One blogger in particular, Susannah Tarbush of *The Tanjara* blog, encouraged me to start sending the longer descriptions and accounts to mainstream media. Emboldened by this, my colleague Jim Hinks and I started to crowd-source volunteer translators from around the world. Quickly a small team emerged for turning around reports for the Western press, and over thirty accounts, diary pieces, and stories were published around the world through various media outlets and in several languages. It is thanks largely to the translators that these ever made it through: namely, Sarah Irving, Ibtihal Mahmood, Elisabeth Jaquette, Thoraya El-Rayyes, Andrew Leber, Ghada Mourad, Tyson Patros, and Orsola Casagrande. Original contributors to *The Book of Gaza* were joined by other writers from across the Strip (including the brilliant seventeen-year-old Rana Mourtaja), and for a brief moment this minuscule, indie publisher of short stories became a conduit for unparalleled eyewitness accounts from a warzone supposedly under the world's spotlight.[3]

At the forefront of these pieces were Atef's own accounts from 2014, which appeared first online (*Slate*, *Guernica*), then in print (the *Sunday Times*, 27 July; a five-page piece in the *Guardian*, 28 July; and an op-ed piece in the *New York Times*, 4 August). This last was a breath of fresh air, given the tacit support for Israel's foreign policy from the *New York Times*' editorial board. Atef's piece polarized reactions among its readers—from Noam Chomsky, in an interview for *Democracy Now*,[4] citing it as an example of how the media's relationship with Israel was changing, to Rabbi Richard A. Block's announcement that he was cancelling his subscription to the *Times*, after a lifetime of reading it.[5]

Unlike the book's other contributors, Atef had been keeping a diary all along. He explained that keeping a diary was one of his traditions of war, a survival ritual. He had kept one for every war so far. He wrote each morning in Arabic, by hand, and it never occurred to him that anyone would read them. Around 21 July, I suggested that he start writing his diary directly in English, which he did. Only when the war was over, did he go back to the earlier Arabic entries to translate them into English.

Editing and distributing these accounts was a disquieting experience, made all the more sad by the fact that what Comma had intended with the earlier anthology—to present a vision of everyday Gaza—was being eroded and replaced by "war writing" from the very authors we had worked with to do the opposite. It also made me see my own motivations with regard to the earlier book more clearly. I had thought that to engender support and empathy for a city, you first had to make Western readers more familiar with it as a landscape, make them feel that they have mentally inhabited it, in some small way. When the city of Bhopal lost 3,787 lives to the Union Carbide disaster, in 1984, the simplest form of justice, compensation, went undelivered for years (it took five years before the owners paid a litigation settlement). But when fewer people died in New York in 2001 (nearly three thousand lives), the entire world changed overnight. The difference wasn't just about power, it seemed to me, but familiarity. Unlike the remote shanty towns of Bhopal, every street corner of Manhattan is iconic to us; millions of people around the world feel they have mentally inhabited New York at some point, even those who've never once visited it. My rather naïve idea with *The Book of Gaza* was to try to inch the city ever so slightly closer to a state of familiarity, to establish it as a place and not just a name, through the simple details that a city's literature brings with it—the referencing of street names, the name-dropping of landmarks and districts. I wanted to start this process, at least.

My motivation was misguided, of course. There is no stability in Gaza on which to build a reader-familiarity, let alone an iconography. Areas that might be iconic in the author's imagination—Jabalia Camp, say, for Atef—lack the long-standing points of reference other cities enjoy. Jabalia Camp is a tangle of hundreds of streets and alleyways—some of them only a couple of feet wide—that have solidified out of years of chaos and overcrowding. Only a handful of the streets even have a name.

As Atef explains (pp. 177–78), buildings and landmarks come and go so quickly in Gaza, being obliterated with each new war, that there is no sense of a static geography to this city, named or unnamed. Indeed it is often the more official, potentially iconic landmarks that have the shortest life expectancy. Areas like the Saraya Crossroad, Tel al-Hawa district, or al-Ansar district have seen two or three generations of potentially iconic landmarks come and go in less than a decade. How can any literature get a purchase on this landscape in the writer's imagination, when the landscape itself doesn't have any long-term purchase on the Palestinian soil?

On his 2014 UK book tour, Atef explained how Gaza's literary life underwent a reboot in 1967 when all the established authors left the Strip. In the immediate aftermath, the subsequent generation of authors rooted their narratives squarely in the past: the towns and villages of their childhood or their parents' generation, the territories lost to them, preserved only in memory and the dream of a return. It was the past that provided the setting (and to some degree the subject) of their stories, rather than the very temporary, fluid landscape of present-day Gaza.

It's perhaps only Atef's generation (writers like Talal Abu Shawish, Yusra al-Khatib, etc.) that glimpsed the possibility of a stable landscape—emerging as they did in the mid '90s, a brief moment of peace and prosperity for the Strip, and managing to bring some of the physicality of Gaza into their stories. If *The Book of Gaza* is anything to go by, however, the subsequent generation seems to have retreated, a little, from writing about the physical space "outside"; authors like Mona Abu Sharekh, Najlaa Ataalah, and Nayrouz Qarmout present the Gazan experience through more internal narratives, inner monologues, and secret correspondences. Perhaps this is simply a result of them still being young as authors. But I worry there might be another cause: that the concrete landscape has been cursed with all the transience of the canvas landscape it replaced, which leaves only war journalists to describe the physical city to the rest of the world, taking us full circle.

I cannot really add to the tragedies that Atef chronicles in these pages. There's little more to say about the atrocities he witnesses. I can point readers towards emerging theories about the long-term Israeli policies behind it—the plan to unseat Hamas before Palestine is able to reap the benefits of recently discovered off-shore oil fields (as exposed by Nafeez Ahmed, shortly before he was sacked by the *Guardian*).[6] Or, I can speculate about an equally gloomy future (the US Army's own Strategic Studies Institute recently recommended extensive US military support for Israel to "manage possible future conflict" over the new-found oil reserves).[7] But the corporate drivers behind state-led genocide are for others to comment on. More important than the personal motives of the political elites is the means by which the Israeli state and Zionists around the world manage to justify this war to themselves and others, the psychology that makes such a moral self-delusion possible. A key tactic of this psychology is to invoke the impunity of any Jewish state—any criticism of the Israeli government is de facto guilty of anti-Semitism. This is a kind of historical hysteria that cannot be argued with as it doesn't come from any evidence-based rationale. Political analysis, even investigative journalism, can only go so far with it; inevitably both will be met with counter theories and even more hysterical self-righteousness. Perhaps the only way forward is to press "pause" on politics altogether and simply listen to Palestinians' testimonies: listen to what they went through and what they're continuing to go through. Until we hear them, until they're genuinely part of the wider conversation, there's nothing to stop the crimes of last summer being committed again.

—*Ra Page, Manchester, February 2015*

SPECIAL THANKS

AS WELL AS the above-mentioned translators and bloggers, the publishers would also like to thank the following for their support in the creation of this book: Alison Boyle, Claire Chambers, Samantha Clark, Mohammed Ghalayini, Christine Gilmore, Peter Florence, Daisy Kidd, Sally Oliver, Nora Parr, Omar Qattan, Wasseem el-Sarraj, Lin and Jon Shaffer, Isaac Shaffer, Trudi Shaw, and, in particular, Pam Bailey.

NOTES

SUNDAY, 6 JULY

1. First Intifada: December 1987–September 1993.
2. Fayza Ahmad (1934–1983), an Egyptian-Syrian singer and actress.
3. Jabalia Camp is the largest of Gaza's eight refugee camps (see p. 18), located north of Gaza City, close to a village of the same name. After the Arab-Israeli war in 1948, 35,000 refugees settled in the camp, most having fled from villages in southern Palestine. Today, nearly 110,000 registered refugees live in the camp, which covers an area of only 1.4 square km.
4. Bureij Camp is located in the center of the Strip east of the Salah al-Din Road in the Deir al-Balah Governorate (see p. 72). The camp was established in 1949 with a population of 13,000 Palestinians from the broader Gaza area. A small percentage of these refugees were housed in the site's British army barracks, but the majority lived in tents, which the UN replaced with concrete homes in 1950. In 2005, Al Bureij had a population of 34,951 with 28,770 registered refugees.
5. *Suhoor*: the pre-dawn, pre-fast meal during Ramadan, around 3 a.m. at this time of year.
6. *Awama*: sweet, fried dough balls not dissimilar to donuts.
7. *Kenafeh*: a cheese pastry soaked in sugar-based syrup, made out of layers of filo pastry; the cheese is typically *Nabulsi* cheese, after the Palestinian city, Nablus.
8. *Katayef*: a popular Ramadan sweet consisting of a small pancake cooked on one side then folded over pistachios and other nuts and served coated in syrup.

MONDAY, 7 JULY

1. On the corner of Omar al-Mukhtar Street and al-Jala'a Street. See p. 202.
2. *Wadi*: an Arabic term for a riverbed or valley that only carries a stream during times of heavy rain.

TUESDAY, 8 JULY

1. *Toktok*: A three-wheeled miniature taxi.

WEDNESDAY, 9 JULY

1. Saed Bannoura, "Offensive Ongoing: Two Women, Two Children, and a Journalist Killed in Gaza," International Middle East Media Center, 10 July 2014, http://www.imemc.org/article/68406_1404949025.

2. "In Memory: Mohammad and Hanaa Malake," *Humanize Palestine* (blog), 9 July 2014, http://humanizepalestine.com/2014/07/09/in-memory-mohammad -hanaa-malake/.

3. Ever since Israel attacked Gaza's sole power station, in 2006, the capacity of the plant has been greatly limited. Now Gaza's energy is provided by a combination of the plant and energy brought in from Israel and Egypt. Consequently, Gazans have had to get used to rolling blackouts, with the electricity on for eight hours, then off for the next eight, and so on. During wars, of course, electricity is even more scarce.

THURSDAY, 10 JULY

1. After the song by the Lebanese singer Fairuz (Nouhad Wadi Haddad).

FRIDAY, 11 JULY

1. Middle East Broadcasting Center, which operates TV stations across the Arab world.

2. Palestinian solidarity groups around the world often distribute random Gazan phone numbers to members so that they might ring and express support during crises.

SUNDAY, 13 JULY

1. "Air Raid of the Air Force on Sheikh Radwan Lead [*sic*] to the Killing of Seven Palestinians," Israel Broadcasting Authority, 7 July 2014, http://www.iba.org.il /arabil/arabic.aspx?entity=1025561&type=1&topic=0.

2. "Father of 4 Year Old Sahar Salman Abu Namous Begs His Son to Wake Up and See the Toy He Bought Him," YouTube, 13 July 2014, https://www.youtube.com /watch?v=d-ouISPCYt4.

3. United Nations Relief and Works Agency.

MONDAY, 14 JULY

1. Dedicated to the Al Aqsa Mosque in Jerusalem.

TUESDAY, 15 JULY

1. Established in 1995 and based in Ramallah, *Al-Ayyam* is the second-largest circulation daily newspaper in the Palestinian territories.

2. A quarterly magazine devoted to Palestinian politics, published by the Institute for Public Policy in Ramallah.

3. Shuja'iyya is one of Gaza City's largest neighborhoods with over one hundred thousand residents. To the southeast of the city center, it is situated around a hill on the Salah al-Din Road that runs the length of the Strip.

WEDNESDAY, 16 JULY

1. "In Memory: Lama Al Satari," *Humanize Palestine* (blog), 15 July 2014, http:// humanizepalestine.com/2014/07/15/in-memory-lama-al-satari/.

2. Leslie Bravery, "Israel's Daily Toll on Palestinian Life, Limb, Liberty and Property," New Zealand Palestine Human Rights Campaign, 16 July 2014, http:// palestine.org.nz/phrc/index.php?option=com_content&task=view&id=2044 &Itemid=44.

THURSDAY, 17 JULY

1. At the junction of Omar al-Mukhtar and Fehmi Bek streets, in Al-Saha (Al-Balad) area.

2. The nine activists killed when Israeli soldiers boarded the lead ship in the Free Gaza Flotilla on 31 May 2010, whilst still in international waters. The flotilla was organized by the Free Gaza Movement and the Turkish Humanitarian Relief Foundation (IHH) and was carrying humanitarian aid and

construction materials, with the intention of breaking the Israeli blockade of the Strip.
3. The phoenix is the symbol of Gaza City.

FRIDAY, 18 JULY

1. Mahmoud Darwish (13 March 1941–9 August 2008) is arguably Palestine's best-known writer, a national poet, a symbol of Palestinian resistance, and a spokesman for Arab opposition to Israeli occupation, generally. His many prizes included the Lotus Prize (Union of Afro-Asian Writers, 1969), the Lenin Peace Prize (USSR, 1983), the Knight of the Order of Arts and Letters (France, 1993), and the Lannan Foundation Prize for Cultural Freedom (2001).
2. Lines from "The Eternity of Cactus," from the collection *Why Have You Left the Horse Alone?*, trans. Jeffrey Sacks (New York: Archipelago, 2006).
3. Literally, the "Bedouin Village."
4. The third largest of the Strip's eight refugee camps, and one of the most crowded, al-Shati' is also known as "Beach Camp." Initially accommodating twenty-three thousand refugees who fled from Lydd, Jaffa, Be'er Sheva, and other areas of Palestine, it is now home to more than eighty-seven thousand refugees, all of whom reside in an area of only 0.52 square kilometers. See p. 72.
5. Now called "Al Ahli Arab Hospital," located on Palestine Square.
6. Situated in the Negev desert, forty-five miles southwest of Be'er Sheva (Beersheba), Ktzi'ot is the largest detention camp in the world. According to Human Rights Watch, in 1990 it held approximately one out of every fifty West Bank or Gazan males over the age of sixteen. Palestinians know it as "Ansar III" after a similar Israeli prison camp set up during the South Lebanon conflict (1982–2000).

SATURDAY, 19 JULY

1. Being so central, and at the furthest distance from any border, Jabalia is presumed by many to be one of the safest areas. It also has a high concentration of UNRWA schools, offering temporary refuge.
2. Sheikh Radwan lies three kilometers to the northwest of Gaza City center, bordering Nasser district to the west, Saftawi to the north, and Jabalia town to the east.

WEDNESDAY, 23 JULY

1. Water shortages in Gaza are a consequence of many factors: fuel shortages, due to the blockade, mean water cannot always be pumped out of wells. Insufficient wastewater treatment (especially after the bombing of wastewater treatment facilities during Operation Cast Lead) has meant nitrogen and chloride levels in the water of Gaza's one aquifer have risen, making 90 to 95 percent of Gaza's main water supply unfit for drinking. "Water Crisis in Gaza Strip: Over 90% of Water Un-potable," B'Tselem, Israeli Information Center for Human Rights in the Occupied Territories, 6 February 2014, http://www.btselem.org/gaza_strip /gaza_water_crisis.

THURSDAY, 24 JULY

1. The United Nations Fact Finding Mission on the Gaza Conflict, established in April 2009 by the UN Human Rights Council during the Gaza war, released its report, known as the Goldstone Report, in September of that year.

FRIDAY, 25 JULY

1. Set in the middle of the Gaza Strip, near both Bureij and Maghazi camps, Nuseirat Camp takes its name from a local Bedouin tribe. Initially it

accommodated sixteen thousand refugees who fled from the southern districts of Palestine after the 1948 Arab-Israeli war, including the coast and Be'er Sheva. Before the camp was formed, refugees had to live in a former British military prison in the area. It is currently home to more than sixty-six thousand refugees. See p. 72.

TUESDAY, 29 JULY

1. "The [question] 'how' [does Israel send these messages] is technologically quite simple to answer. The entirety of the Palestinian telecommunications infrastructure is one that is dependent, reliant, and subservient to Israel's, both in Gaza and the West Bank. [. . .] There is a Palestinian telecommunications provider: Paltel. It boasts a cellular subsidiary firm, Jawwal, and an internet provider, Hadara. But for all intents and purposes Paltel is a reseller of Israeli telecommunications capacity. Every phone call made within Gaza, between Gaza and the West Bank, and between Gaza and the rest of the world, for example, is physically wired through Israel. [. . .] Palestinians subscribers pay for their land-line, cellular, and internet use directly to Paltel and its subsidiaries. Paltel in turn pays for its telecommunications capacity that it purchases from Israeli providers. There is no other choice. Israel does not permit Paltel to purchase internet capacity from neighboring Jordan or Egypt for example. And Paltel has equally not been permitted by Israeli authorities to have its own international connections." Helga Tawil-Souri, "Israel's Warnings: TechnoPolitics," *Digital Occupation* (blog), 17 July 2014, http://helga.com/blog/?p=22.

FRIDAY, 1 AUGUST

1. The delegation was led by Azam al Ahmad and included Mosa Abu Marzouk, Khalil al-Haya, Zyad al-Nakhala, and Majid Faraj.

MONDAY, 4 AUGUST

1. An anthology the author edited for Comma Press in 2014. See pp. 241–247.

SATURDAY, 9 AUGUST

1. The PNA was the (supposedly) interim self-governing body established to govern Gaza and two of the three West Bank areas as a consequence of the 1993 Oslo Accords. Although Hamas has controlled Gaza since 2007, the government infrastructure in Gaza is still referred to, internally, as the PNA. The curriculum in PNA-run schools is much the same as it was before 2007.

SUNDAY, 10 AUGUST

1. "Strike at Gaza School 'Kills 40,'" BBC News, January 7, 2009, http://news.bbc .co.uk/1/hi/world/middle_east/7814054.stm.

MONDAY, 11 AUGUST

1. "Madeeh al-Thill al-'Aaly" ("In Praise of High Shadow").
2. Ghassan Kanafani (1936–1972) was a Palestinian novelist and leading member of the Popular Front for the Liberation of Palestine. His novels include *Men in the Sun* (1963), *All That's Left of You* (1966), and *Return to Haifa* (1970). He was a major modernizing influence on Arab literature and an early proponent of complex narrative structures, using flashback effects and a chorus of different narrative voices. He was assassinated (along with his seventeen-year-old niece, Lamees Najim) by a Mossad car bomb.

SATURDAY, 16 AUGUST

1. An Arabic version of the card game rummy.

THURSDAY, 21 AUGUST

1. "Israel Killed His Parents Thursday, Lawyer Younis: Signing Rome Statute Is Must," *Al Ray Palestinian Media Agency*, August 22, 2014, http://alray.ps/en/index.php?act=post&id=5191#.Vd3CthRVhBd.

SATURDAY, 23 AUGUST

1. According to a report by the Ministry of Health's Information Center in Ramallah, published February 2013, cancer was responsible for 12.4 percent of deaths in Palestine in 2013, compared to 10.8 percent in 2012. (Asmaa al-Ghoul, "Gaza Cancer Rates on Rise," *Al-Monitor*, 1 April 2013, http://www.al-monitor.com/pulse/originals/2013/03/cancer-rates-soar-gaza-war.html.)

2. Ali Abunimah, "'Gaza's 9/11': Israel Destroys High-Rise Building in Gaza—Video," *The Electronic Intifada* (blog), 23 August 2014, http://electronicintifada.net/blogs/ali-abunimah/gazas-911-israel-destroys-high-rise-building-gaza-video.

MONDAY, 25 AUGUST

1. Ahmad Dahbour, born 1946 in Haifa.

TUESDAY, 26 AUGUST

1. The hundred or so fishermen allowed out to sea are restricted often to only three kilometers out, although occasionally this is extended to six.

AFTERWORD

1. The terms of the cease-fire agreed to by all parties on 26 August 2014 were never officially published or otherwise shared, which makes it almost impossible to enforce accountability. However, it is generally agreed that they included a) a multilateral cease-fire; b) the opening of the crossings into and out of Gaza; c) an extension of the fishing limit off Gaza's coast from three to six miles, with discussions in one month about extending it further; d) a reduction of the "security zone" inside Gaza from three hundred meters to one hundred; and e) a resumption of Egyptian-brokered talks by 26 September to discuss the release of prisoners, the opening of a seaport and/or airport, and other remaining issues. None of these commitments, however, have been fulfilled. The Israeli crossings into and out of Gaza have opened somewhat more than previously, in part to make up for the total closure of Egypt's Rafah crossing, but are nowhere near fully open. And no further talks regarding a lifting of the blockade have been held, in part due to the failure of the Palestinian unity government (reuniting Fatah and Hamas) to solidify. More here: "Gaza Conflict: Israel and Palestinians Agree Long-Term Truce," BBC News, 27 August 2014, http://www.bbc.com/news/world-middle-east-28939350.

2. The UN Relief and Works Agency (UNRWA) announced on 27 January 2015 that it would stop aiding Palestinian families whose homes were destroyed in the Israeli offensive due to a shortfall in the expected donations from international donors. In a statement, UNRWA said it had only received US$135 million out of $724 million pledged. "Lack of Funds Forces UNRWA to Suspend Cash Assistance for Repairs to Damaged and Destroyed Homes in Gaza," 27 January 2015, UNRWA.org.

3. In its weekly report, issued on 26 January 2015, the UN Office for the Coordination of Humanitarian Affairs (OCHA) stated that around twelve thousand internally displaced persons were still sheltering in UNRWA-administered centers across the Gaza Strip. As of May 2015, OCHA estimated that more than one hundred thousand people remain displaced in precarious and vulnerable conditions.

4. By early January 2015, according to OCHA, nearly forty thousand Gaza residents had been granted authorization to purchase construction materials restricted under the Israeli blockade; however, fewer than 40 percent of them had actually been able to afford to do so.

5. The latter two are titles of pro-Palestinian songs by the Lebanese composer and singer Marcel Khalifa.

6. In the week of 20 January alone, reports OCHA, at least thirteen incidents occurred in which Israeli naval forces opened fire at Palestinian fishing boats, reportedly sailing within the Israeli-declared six-nautical-mile fishing limit.

7. With Egypt joining Israel in harshly controlling use of border crossings by Palestinians, a growing number of Palestinians of Gaza believe an open seaport is their only hope of true independence and freedom.

EDITOR'S NOTE TO THE UK EDITION

1. As reported by the BBC journalist Jon Donnison via Twitter: "Israeli police Mickey Rosenfeld Yes tells me men who killed 3 Israeli teens def lone cell, hamas affiliated but not operating under leadership," @JonDonnison, 25 July 2014, 5:45 p.m. More here: Katie Zavadski, "It Turns Out Hamas May Not Have Kidnapped and Killed the 3 Israeli Teens After All," *Daily Intelligencer* blog, *New York* magazine, 25 July 2014, http://nymag.com/daily/intelligencer/2014/07/hamas-didnt-kidnap-the-israeli-teens-after-all.html.

2. A full list of these messages can be found on the Comma Press blog: https://thecommapressblog.wordpress.com/2014/07/23.

3. A full list of links to these articles can be found here: http://commapress.co.uk/books/the-book-of-gaza.

4. Amy Goodman, "Noam Chomsky: Israel's Actions in Palestine Are 'Much Worse Than Apartheid' in South Africa," transcription, *Democracy Now*, 8 August 2014, http://www.democracynow.org/blog/2014/8/8/noam_chomsky_what_israel_is_doing.

5. Richard A. Block, "Why I'm Unsubscribing from the *New York Times*," *Tablet*, 28 August 2014, http://tabletmag.com/scroll/183412/why-im-unsubscribing-to-the-new-york-times.

6. Original blog: Nafeez Ahmed, "IDF's Gaza Assault Is to Control Palestinian Gas, Avert Israeli Energy Crisis," 9 July 2014, *Guardian*, http://www.theguardian.com/environment/earth-insight/2014/jul/09/israel-war-gaza-palestine-natural-gas-energy-crisis. Comment on his removal from the *Guardian*: Jonathan Cook, "Why the Guardian Axed Nafeez Ahmed's Blog," *Jonathan Cook*, 4 December 2014, http://www.jonathan-cook.net/blog/2014-12-04/why-the-guardian-axed-nafeez-ahmeds-blog/.

7. Original study: Laura El-Katiri and Mohammed El-Katiri, *Regionalizing East Mediterranean Gas: Energy Security, Stability, and the US Role* (Carlisle, PA: Strategic Studies Institute and US Army War College Press, December 2014), www.strategicstudiesinstitute.army.mil/pdffiles/PUB1243.pdf. Comment: Nafeez Ahmed, "US Army Report Calls for 'Military Support' of Israeli Energy Grab," *Middle East Eye*, 1 January 2015, http://www.middleeasteye.net/columns/us-army-report-calls-military-support-israeli-energy-grab-57185571.

Printed in the United States
by Baker & Taylor Publisher Services